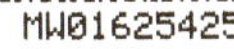

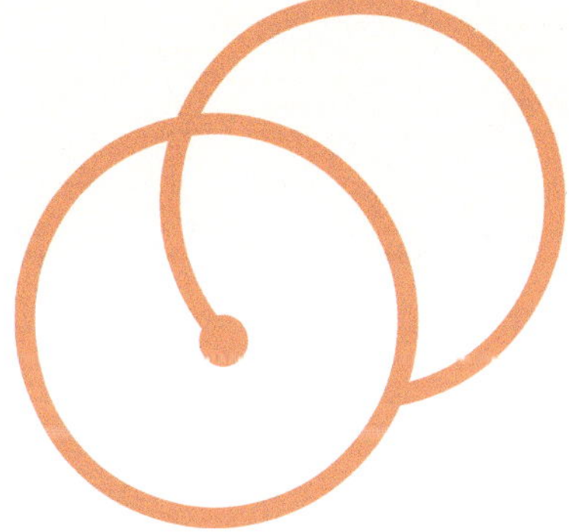
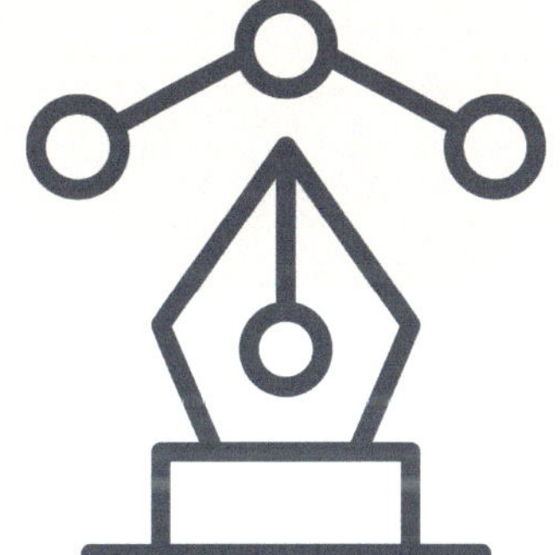
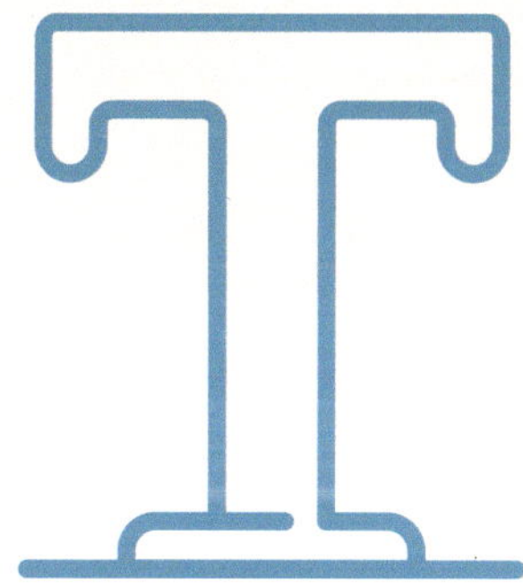

LOGO DESiGN
Fundamentals

An Introduction & Workbook for Beginners

Including logo design principles, tips, ideas branding, practice projects, and more!

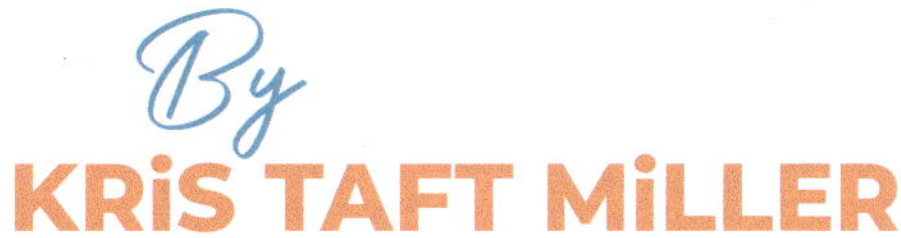

By
KRiS TAFT MiLLER

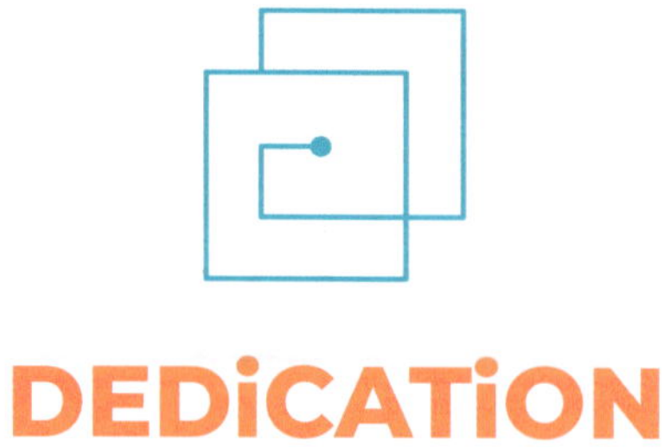

DEDiCATiON

This book is dedicated to my three boys, my two sons and my husband, who are the reason for my everything.

KT Design, LLC
www.ktdesignacademy.com

ISBN: 978-1-7378206-5-9
Imprint: Independently published by KT Design, LLC

TABLE of CONTENTS

Chapter One

WELCOME & iNTRODUCTiON

Welcome!

Hello! My name is Kris, and in case you don't know anything about me here is a quick bio. I started my design career at Walt Disney Feature Animation, where I was lucky enough to spend eight incredible years working on animated films such as *Lilo & Stitch, Brother Bear, Meet the Robinsons, Chicken Little,* and even *Frozen* back when it was called *Snow Queen*, as well as many, many more. I left Disney because I met my husband who lived in North Carolina and decided it was the best time to start my own design agency. It was not the easiest thing to do and I learned a TON that first year. I actually have a degree in education, and all of my graphic design training was on the job at Disney. I have been fortunate enough to establish a successful freelance career for the past 20 years, and I am so looking forward to sharing what I have learned both at Disney and on my own.

The purpose of this book is to provide a beginner level education about logo design. This includes common terms, basic logo design fundamentals, how to find inspiration, fonts (my favorite), and more! Most importantly, I want you to feel like you can jump right in and try your hand at designing a logo!

Copyright

But first we are going to quickly discuss copyright. It is real, and it is important and vital for designers to know and understand what copyright is and how to avoid copyright infringement. If you are drawing inspiration from a resource, then the most important thing to remember in regards to copyright infringement in my opinion is to be CERTAIN to create your own original artwork. If you are utilizing stock artwork, then you need to be comfortable reading the terms of use and how they relate to your project, including what your client intends to use the item for and so on. Logos, for example, should always be your own original work so they can always be trademarked if your client wants to do that.

Bottom line with copyright is: if you are in doubt...ASK. I have emailed resources many times asking for permission to use something or asking for clarification on their terms of use, often referred to as TOU. I know a very successful painter who often draws inspiration for her portraits from modeling images she finds online. She ALWAYS contacts the owner/model and researches how to gain proper permission to use the photograph as inspiration for her paintings.

Ok – enough about that – let's move on to the fun stuff!

Chapter Two

WHAT iS A LOGO?

A logo is a visual representation of the essence of a brand. What is a brand, you say? A brand is "a product, service, or concept that is publicly distinguished from other products, services, or concepts so that it can be easily communicated and, usually, marketed." Or as Jeff Bezos (CEO/ Founder of Amazon) so eloquently put it, "Your brand is what other people say about you when you're not in the room."

A logo is a powerful tool to serve as a visual shortcut to a company's brand.

A logo design and a strong brand definition are both important when marketing a consistent identity for your company or client.

Personally, I like the iceberg analogy, where the brand is the full iceberg, most of it behind the scenes and "invisible," with just a portion of it "visible," and just the tip of the iceberg is the logo.

So this book is about the tip of the iceberg. Let's take a quick look at some of the most iconic logos to get your inspiration peaked.

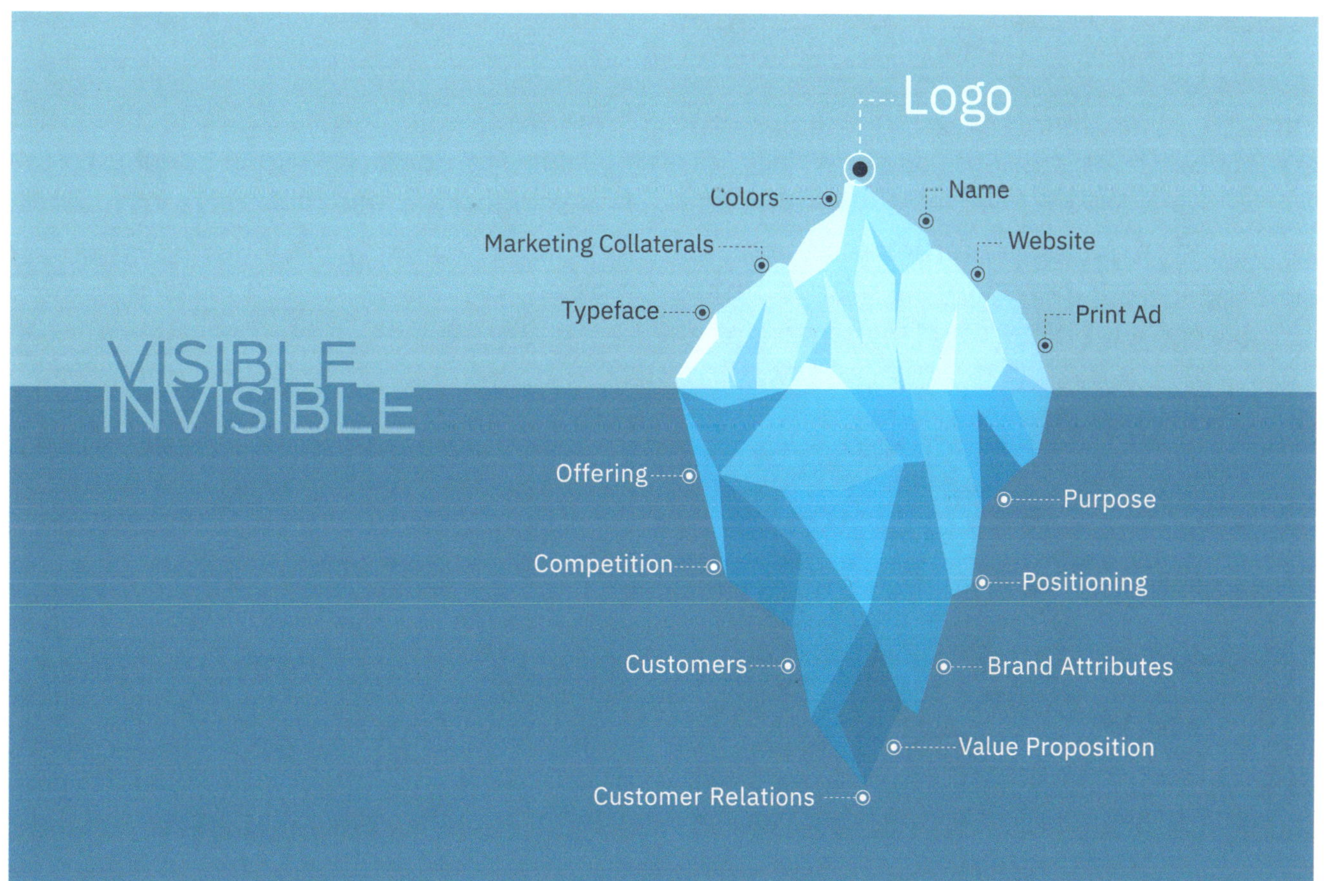

One of the logos that we see the most often is the Amazon logo. This is a great example of a logo that follows the five logo design principles that we will discuss in chapter three.

It is quite simple, memorable with its "a to z" reference and versatile in its ability to be recognizable in any color and at a wide variety of sizes, from an airplane to a box.

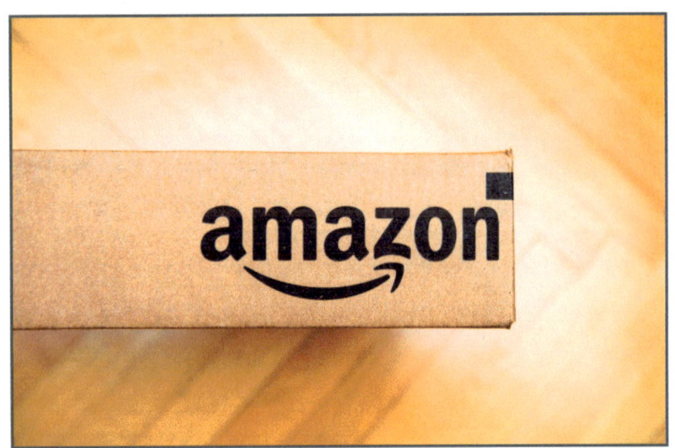

Another awesome example of basic shapes that have been used incredibly effectively to create an iconic visual is this one below with just four squares in four colors.

Do you need me to say it? It is Microsoft, of course. Bold, simple, memorable, versatile, and timeless – this logo design is one to admire.

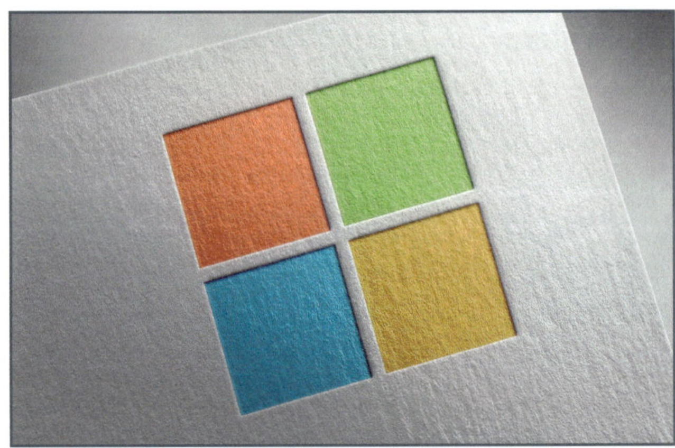

Another logo that is a good example of effective use of the logo design principles is the Target logo. With just two shapes, combined in an iconic target appearance, and the use of the color red, this logo has established itself quite well in modern culture.

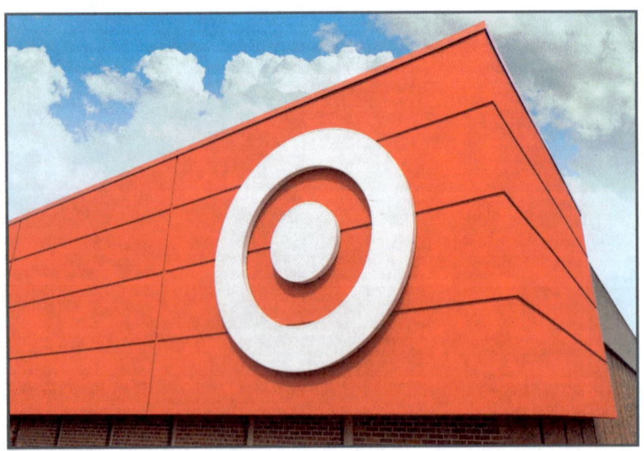

It wouldn't be right to discuss effective logos of major corporations without a nod to the FedEx logo. From the two colors, to the bold font, to the hidden arrow, this logo design has it all.

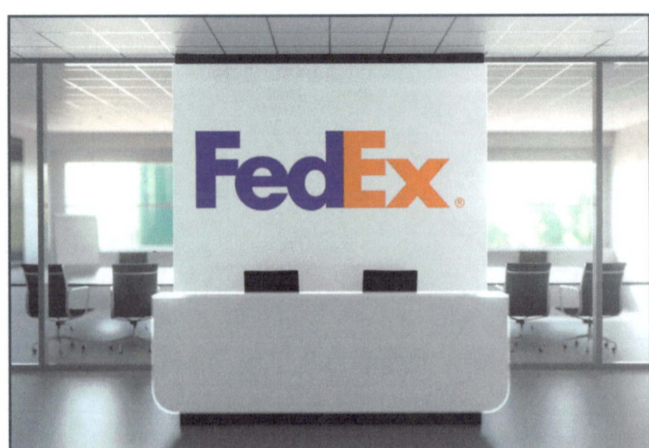

A more complicated logo design that still works on many levels is the Starbucks logo. Whether it is seen in its trademark green color or in black or white, this versatile logo design can truly be used without the brand's name and still be definitively recognizable.

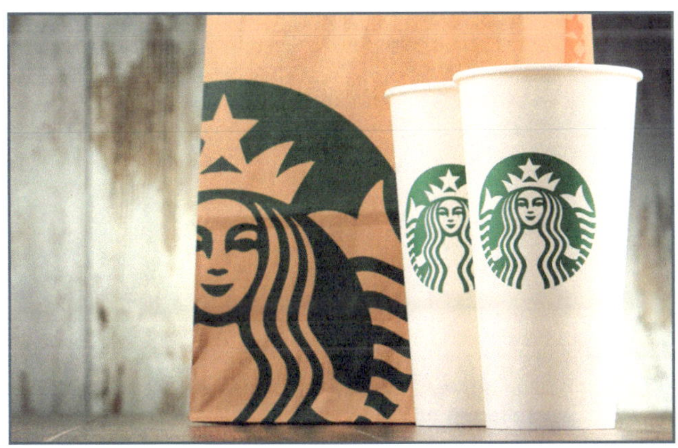

If you have ever played one of those logo games where you have to name the logo without the company name attached, then this one below should be an easy win. Even the description of the golden arches easily and quickly evokes the smell of french fries.

Dating back to the 1960s, the iconic logo design for McDonald's has only changed slightly over the years and still remains one of the most recognizable brands in the world.

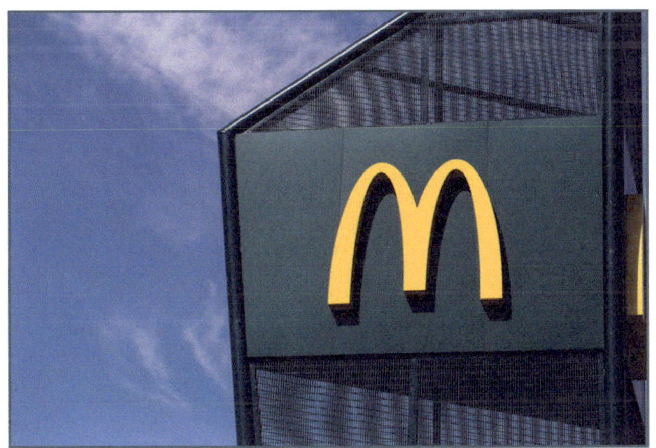

One of my favorite iconic logo designs is the Apple company logo. The epitome of simple, reproducable in any color, with or without the word, and timeless to a tee, this logo should stand the test of time.

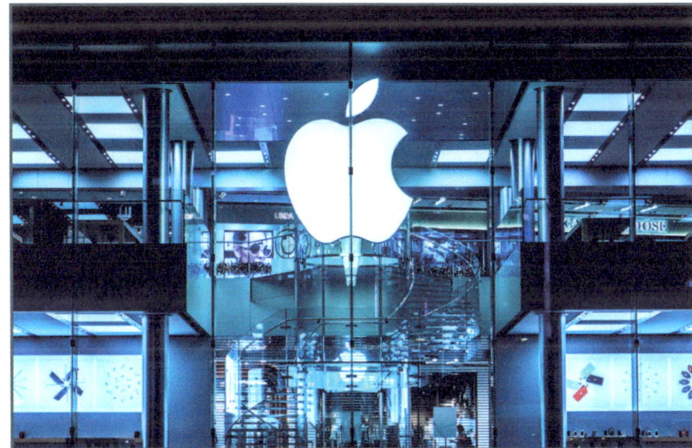

Hopefully your logo design creative juices are flowing freely by now, and you are ready to absorb all of the principles and ideals to keep in mind when approaching a logo design project. Let's move on to breaking down the five main logo design principles.

Chapter Three

THE 5 MAiN PRiNCiPLES OF LOGO DESiGN

Think about all of the logo designs you can identify with just a quick glance, no words necessary, or even just a short description of the visual icon.

For instance, can you close your eyes and bring up the iconic visuals of logo designs of companies such as Nike, Google, or Visa?

To create a logo that is memorable and easy to recognize, try to keep these five main principles in mind.

PRINCIPLE

#1

OF LOGO DESIGN

K.I.S.S.

K.I.S.S. or Keep it simple stupid. This principle is one of easiest to remember and also one of the hardest to achieve. The greatest logo designs are often the most simple. This definitely does not equate to being easily achievable, as simplicity plus effectiveness is a hard line to walk.

Reducing the number of colors and lines in a logo, at least initially, can be helpful to create a simple and effective visual.

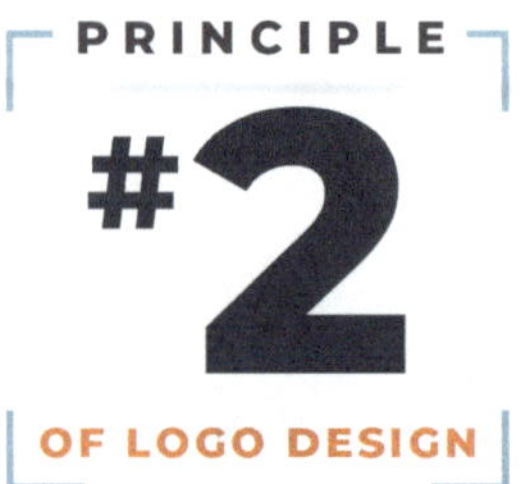

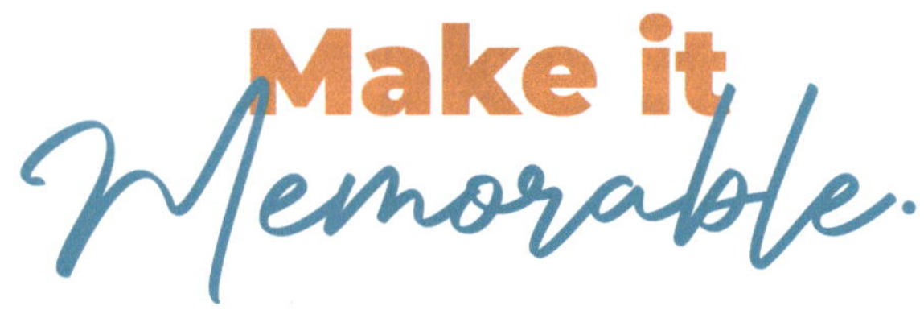

Whatever the brand, it is important that your logo is memorable. This idea goes along with the first one of keeping it simple. Often the more simpler logo designs are easy to remember and almost hard to forget. So if you want to look at it that way, try to aim for a design that is hard to forget.

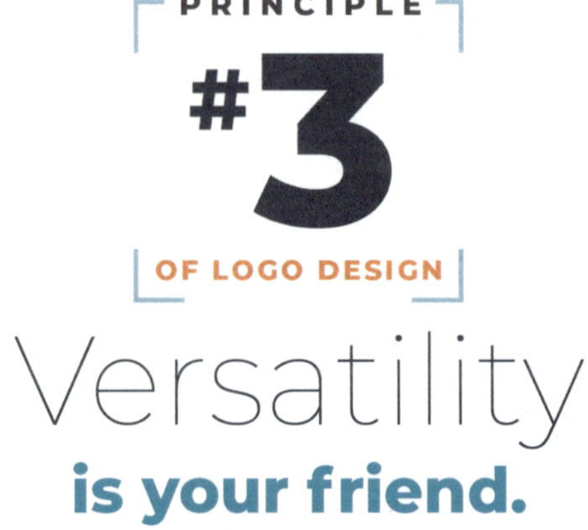

A great logo looks good in a variety of sizes and colors. Your logo should have the versatility to be used on a billboard as well as a button.

A logo design that offers flexibility in areas such as layout (horizontal or vertical), any color or no color, size, and so on, is ideal.

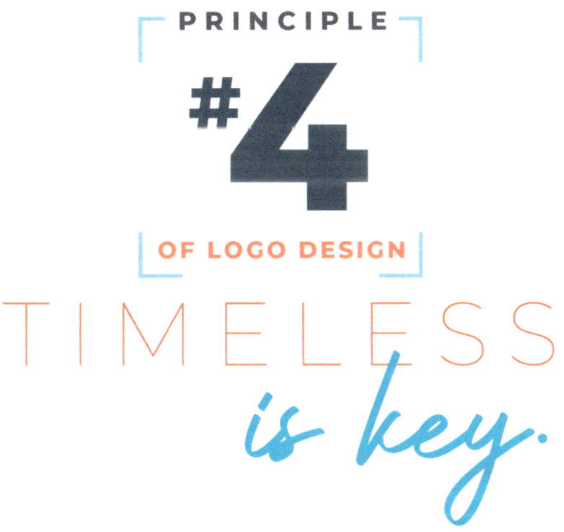

One of the most important factors to consider in logo design is how to make the design's appeal last over time. Yet another reason to aim for a simple and effective design, as these are often what can stand the test of time.

Keeping your logo from feeling dated can be difficult when following any current trends in design, so it is often best to avoid being too "trendy" and instead to try to achieve a timeless look.

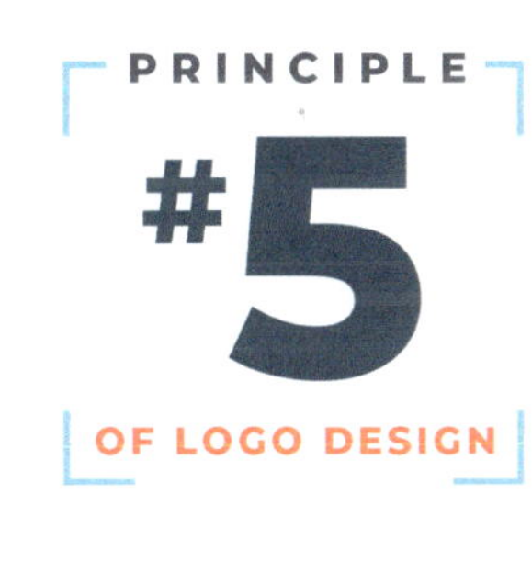

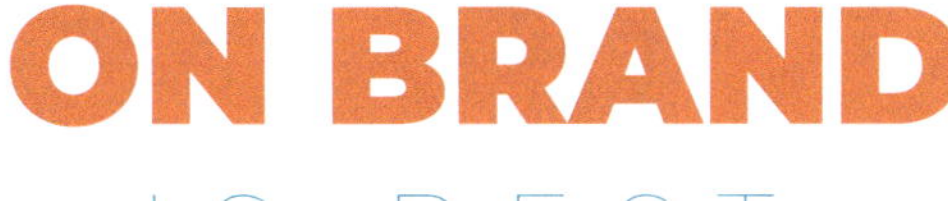

Your logo design should be on brand when dealing with a company that has an established brand. When your logo design is the very first item to be created for a company, be sure to keep in mind that you are essentially establishing the brand with your font, color, and design choices.

The tone and feel of your logo should match the audience that it is intended for. The colors for a kid's activity place would probably not be the same colors as a doctor's office or a pharmaceutical company, and so on.

These five principles are listed on the next page for easy reference to print and post where you can see them.

Let's move on to examing the psychology of logo design and what shapes, colors, fonts, and other design choices that you make might mean for your ultimate final design.

THE 5 PRINCIPLES OF *Logo* DESIGN

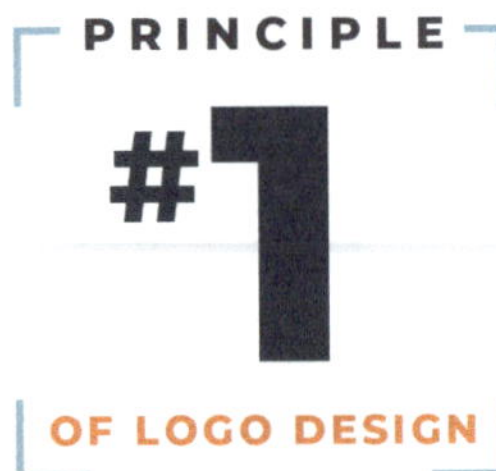

K.I.S.S.

Keep It Simple Stupid.

PRINCIPLE #2 OF LOGO DESIGN

Make it *Memorable.*

PRINCIPLE #3 OF LOGO DESIGN

Versatility **is your friend.**

PRINCIPLE #4 OF LOGO DESIGN

TIMELESS *is key.*

PRINCIPLE #5 OF LOGO DESIGN

ON BRAND IS BEST.

Chapter Four

THE PSYCHOLOGY OF LOGO DESiGN

Any effective logo design can evoke an emotional reaction, even minimally, that is influenced by the use of color, shape, and font within the design. If you look around at all of the recognizable brands that surround us daily, you can examine more closely how each one makes you feel.

These logos and the reactions they cause come from very deliberate design choices made by their branding team or individual. They set out to grab our attention, create an emotional response, and lead us to trust and purchase from the companies behind them.

Although I am someone who likes to dive right in and start designing, it can be important to remember to slow down and take the time to understand the psychology behind your design choices. Ultimately, it should help you create a more memorable and timeless design.

Creating an effective logo design is not as easy as picking your favorite colors or icons and slapping them together...unless that works for you and then good for you - you really don't need to read this chapter. For the rest of you who are interested in what your design choices mean, read on!

Understanding the meaning behind specific shapes and color combinations and what they represent will help you work with more intention and be able to back up your choices with sound reasoning to your clients.

So start with some brand research. Some common questions to start with, and can often be asked directly to your client, are:

- What are you trying to convey with your logo design?
- How do you want people to feel when they see your logo?
- What kind of connections do you want the viewer to make between your logo and your business?
- What are some of your competitor's logo designs, and how do they make you feel?
- What do you like and dislike about your competitor's logos?

Some of the essential elements that make up your logo design are the ***fonts, shapes, colors, lines,*** and ***composition***. Each one of these has a psychology behind it that influences how the audience perceives your logo.

Let's delve in to more detail, and what better place to start than where I always start with a logo design. Fonts.

FONTS

I don't know about you, but I definitely have an emotional reaction to fonts. In fact, all people have a psychological response to fonts, even if most people don't recognize it. The emotional reaction created by a font is tied to the shape of the letters and their "attitude".

What is a font's "attitude"? Think of it as the personality of the font and the tone it sets almost immediately in a design. Check out the font attitudes for a chart of some basic traits people have historically associated with different kinds of fonts.

Above everything else, and I cannot stress this enough, your text should be legible. No one should have to work to read the name of the company in your logo design. The whole goal is to be a recognizable brand so make sure the actual name is recognizable!

SHAPES

Literally everything has a shape. A letter, an icon, an image, everything, and shapes communicate messages whether you realize it or not. Therefore, it is important to understand the messaging you are using in your logo design.

We can break shapes down into three main categories: organic or natural, abstract or symbolic, and geometric or mathematical. Let's examine the psychology of each of these.

Organic or natural shapes are just like you might imagine - often occuring in nature but also including any non-conforming irregular shape that is considered random and free flowing. Organic shapes definitely create an emotional reaction, with natural shapes often eliciting calm and soothing feelings, making them ideal for spas, therapists, etc. Natural shapes with sharp angles may create an anxious reaction, while softer lines tend to create a feeling of relaxation. More abstract shapes are open to the viewer's interpretation, so be careful not to overlook something in an abstract shape that might create a message you did not intend.

Abstract or symbolic shapes are probably most often utilized in logo design. These tend to be basic shapes that represent something familiar to the viewers and quickly convey a message about the company through its logo. Utilizing symbols in a clever capacity is often the goal of a successful logo using this approach.

For instance, using something as simple as an arrow might not be interesting enough in a logo design. However, the use of an arrow in the FedEx logo is considered a brilliant and clever approach. Check out the table on the page about "shapes" for a more comprehensive look at what different symbols can convey.

Geometric of mathematical shapes are just what they sound like - circles, squares, rectangles, triangles, and so on. These shapes tend to be the opposite of organic or natural shapes, as they do not tend to appear in nature and therefore are used to convey a very different emotion. Geometric shapes are typically used to convey stability, strength, order, and reliability, and can provide a more corporate company feel. A more detailed list of what each geometric shape can communicate is included in the "shapes" table on page 20.

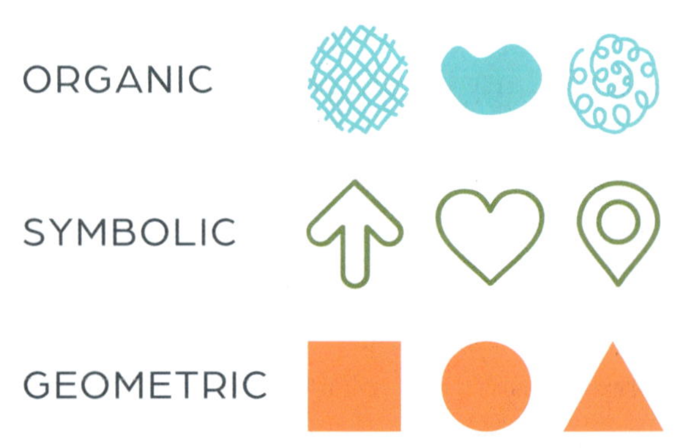

COLORS

Choosing your logo colors can be one of the hardest parts about your design. I once had a client whose wife said he spent far less time deciding on their first child's name than he did on the color of his company's logo. Each color can evoke specific emotions and communicate intentional feelings. The colors you choose for your logo will ultimately represent a major message you are trying to convey in those initial 5–7 seconds you have to catch a person's attention.

Understanding how color can impact the emotinonal response from your audience is an important step in creating an effective logo design. For example, red is associated with power, love, and confidence, to name a few. However, in some cultures red can have negative implications and can convey anger or danger. Red is also very commonly seen in fast food logos, as it is thought to evoke hunger. Look around next time you drive by an area with lots of fast food restaurants, and you will be hard pressed to find a successful one without the color red incorporated in some way.

Color combinations will also impact your design, making it important to understand the relationship between your color choices.

ANALOGOUS COLOR SCHEMES

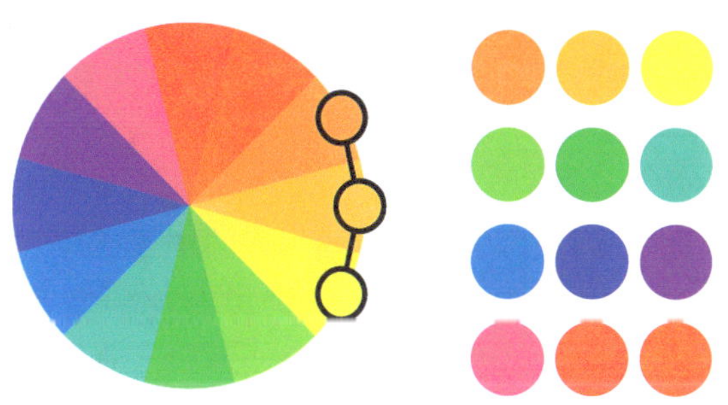

MONOCHROMATIC COLOR SCHEMES

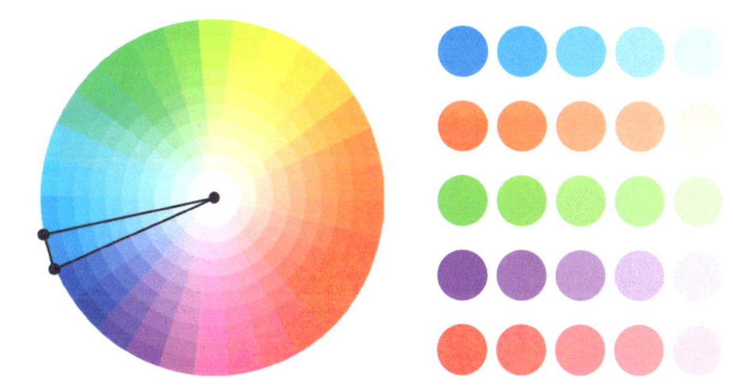

SPLIT COMPLEMENTARY

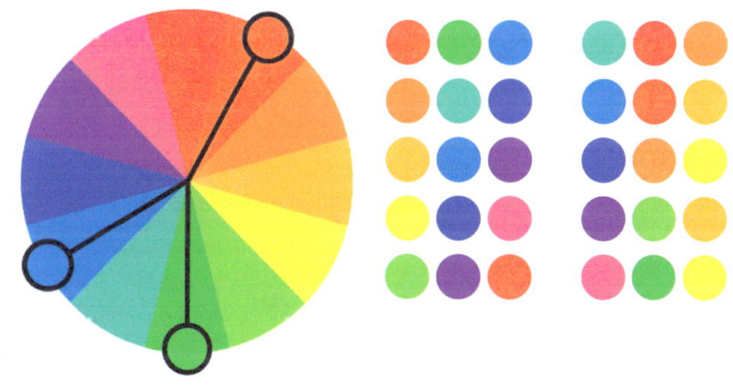

COMPLEMENTARY

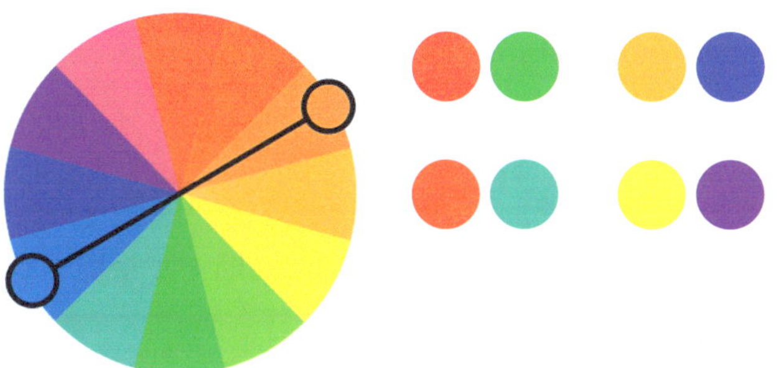

SQUARE COMPLEMENTARY

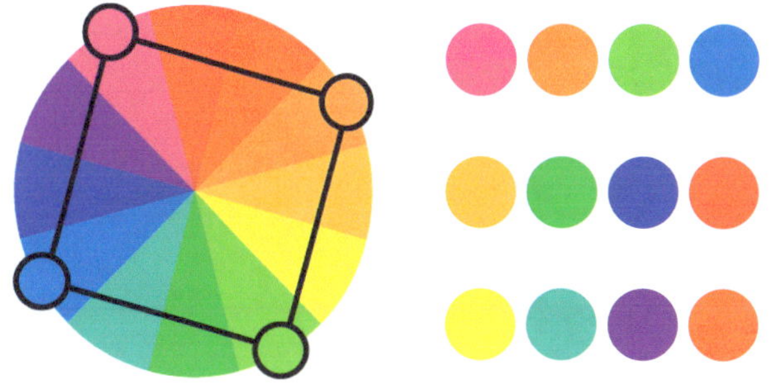

Consider color schemes such as monochromatic, analogous, or complementary to help you choose colors that are proven to work well together.

Keeping with the first logo design principle to keep it simple, you will probably want to limit your logo design to no more than three colors. With any rule there are exceptions, but typically you should be able to convey everything you need to with three colors or less.

Check out the "colors" page to see a more detailed breakdown of emotions that colors can convey.

LINES

Do not underestimate the power of a line. Lines are literally everywhere we look. They communicate everything from where to go to where to look, how to drive, where to stand, and so on. They are the foundation of so much of the visuals we see on a daily basis, and, just like the other elements of a logo design, they have psychological impacts depending on how they are represented.

Thick, thin, straight, curvy, horizontal, vertical, smooth, angular... the list could go on and on. Check out the lines table in the following pages for a more comprehensive breakdown of the different lines and how they can impact your logo designs.

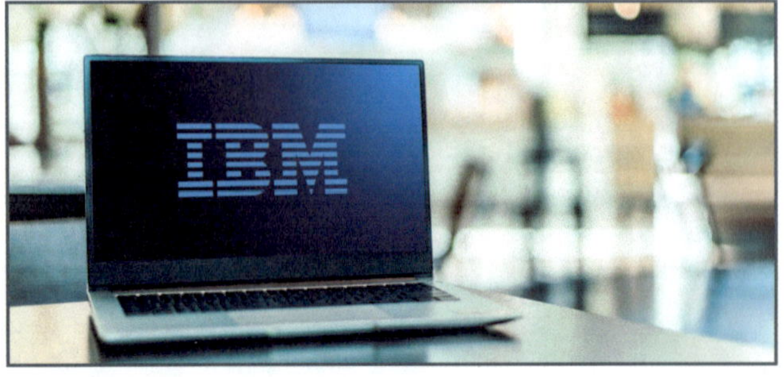

COMPOSITION

Bringing everything together into your final composition is the last powerful tool in your logo design arsenal. Some questions you should ask yourself when composing your logo design are below.

How should each element relate to each other in terms of size to create balance? Size can represent importance, so keep in mind that the larger element in your logo design will be perceived as the most important.

How should my elements align OR not align? How you organize your logo elements will convey a message as well, so make this choice with intention. More scattered items will evoke a more playful feel, while perfectly aligned objects will convey order and stability.

How should I order the elements of my design? Items that are on the left side of the logo will be seen first (at least in the west where we read from left to right), so what element do you want to include all the way to the left?

How should my elements relate to each other? Should there be anything touching, or should there be significant white space between two items, etc. Deciding how each individual element relates to the other is crucial in bringing your logo design together in a cohesive manner. Simply slapping an icon next to a word is often not as effective as somesort of interaction between the different elements in your logo composition.

Considering all of the psychological logo design elements we discussed will help lead you on a path to your next rock star logo design!

FONT *Psychology*

Here are some examples of the emotions communicated by different types of fonts.

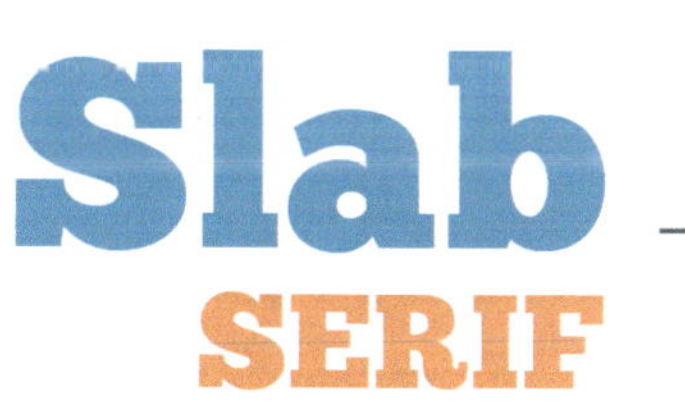

- strong
- solid
- important
- funky
- bold

Sans SERIF

- easy to read
- simple
- clean
- stable
- neutral

Serif

- timeless
- respectable
- formal
- impressive
- traditional

Bold

- significant
- dominant
- fearless
- noble
- dignified

Decorative

- cool
- individual
- rare
- casual
- unique

MODERN SERIF

- luxurious
- glamorous
- polished
- refined
- elegant

Modern SANS SERIF

- unique
- uncommon
- neat
- progressive
- innovative

Italic

- distinct
- fancy
- noticeable
- movement
- action

FONT *Psychology*

Here are some examples of the emotions communicated by different types of fonts.

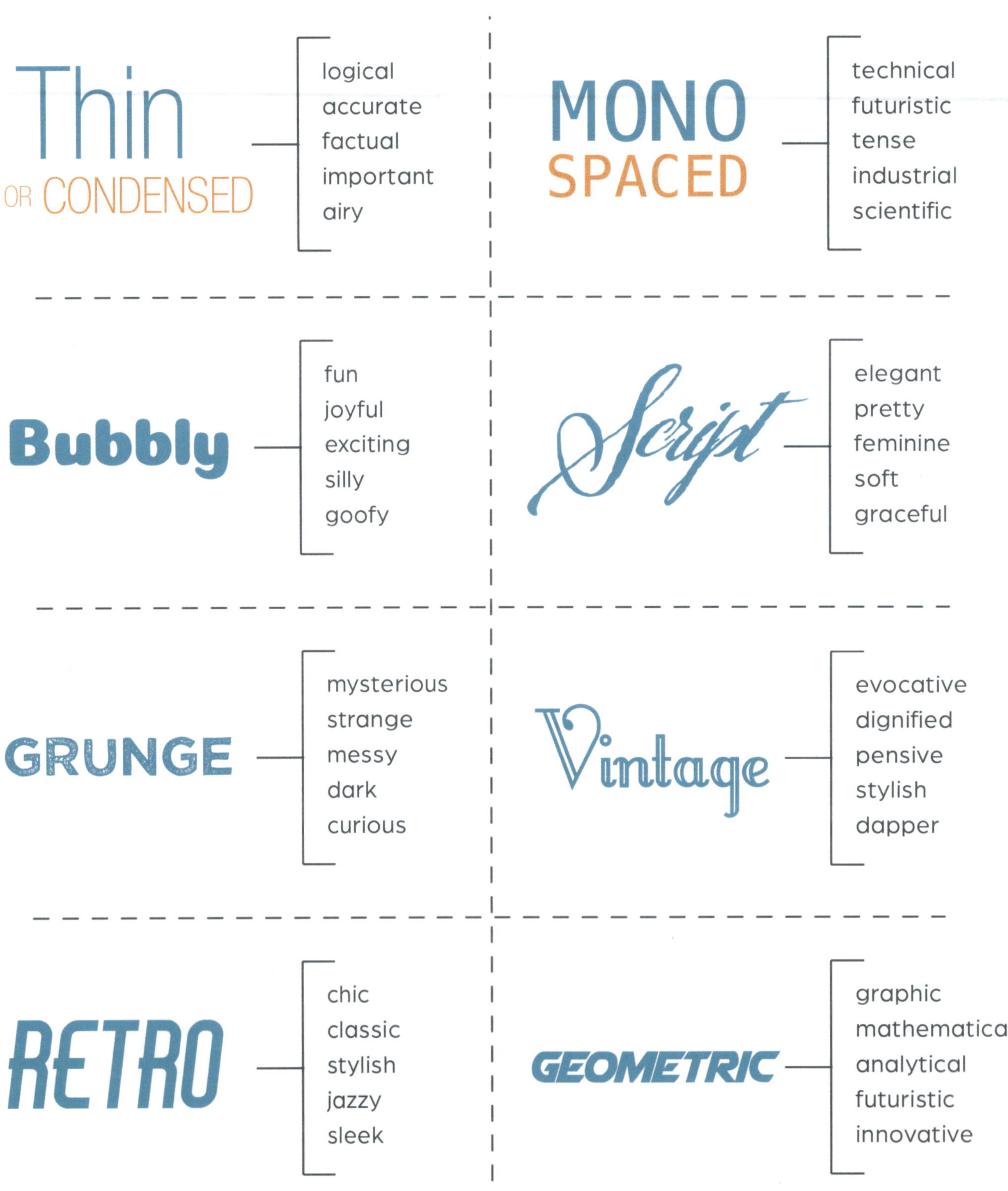

FONT *Psychology*

Here are some examples of the emotions communicated by different types of fonts.

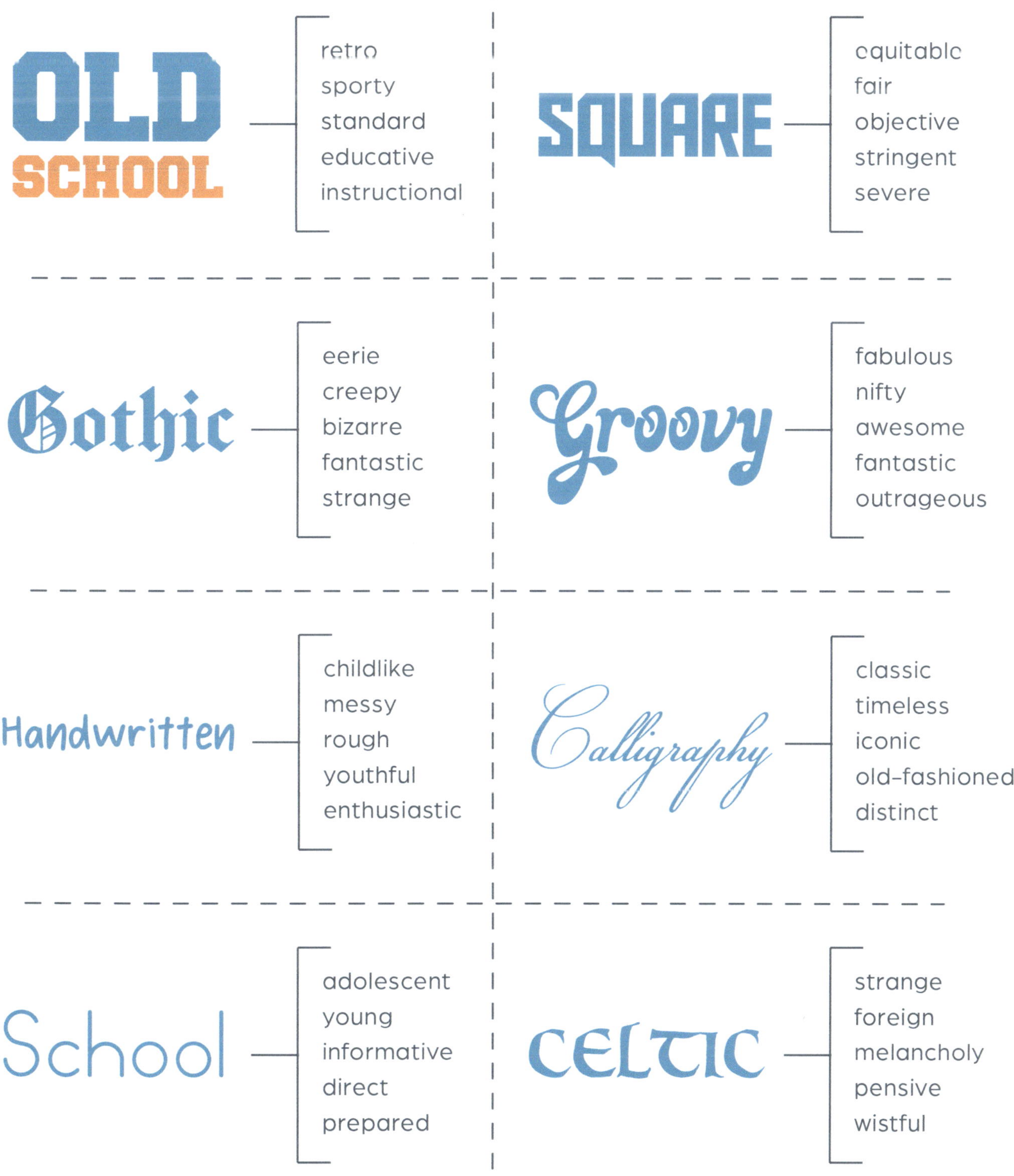

SHAPE Psychology

Logo shapes can be broken down into three main categories.

ORGANIC

Naturally occurring shapes, such as trees, leaves, flowers, and so on, are considered organic shapes. They are typically free form shapes that do not follow any rules and are often asymmetrical and irregular.

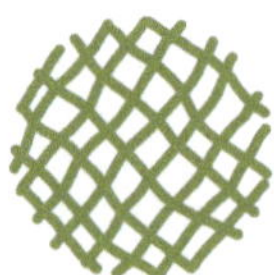
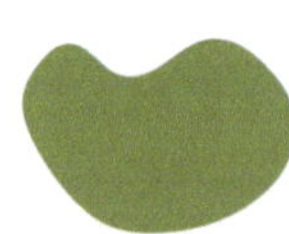
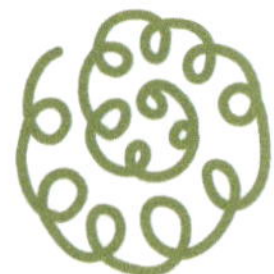

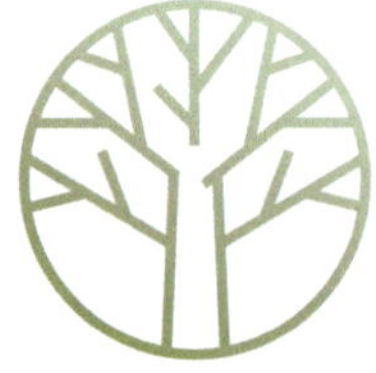

Think of the four **NATURAL** elements–fire, water, earth, and air–for logo inspiration.

Shapes that occur in nature follow **NO SET PATH,** making them adaptable and flexible.

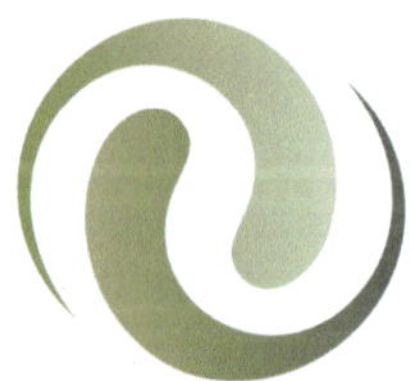
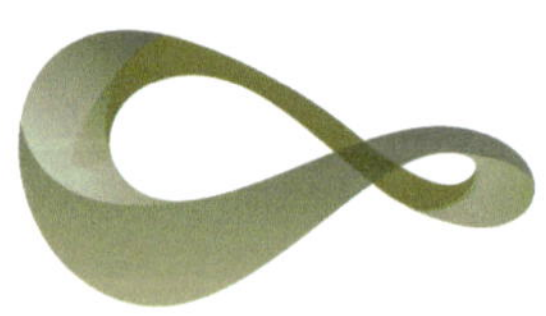

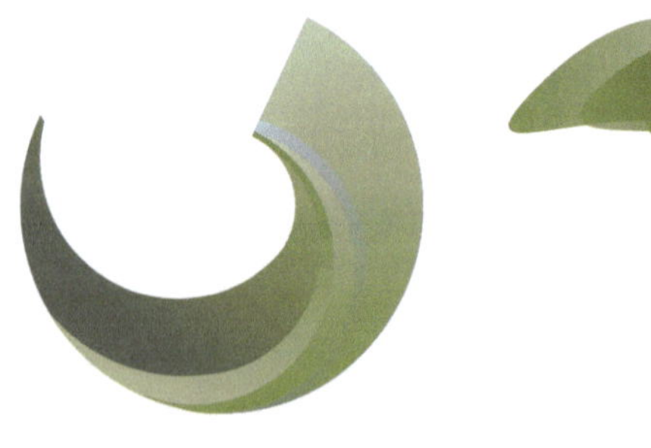

Humans tend to avoid sharp objects, making curved shapes and lines feel safe and inviting, and therefore appealing in logo design.

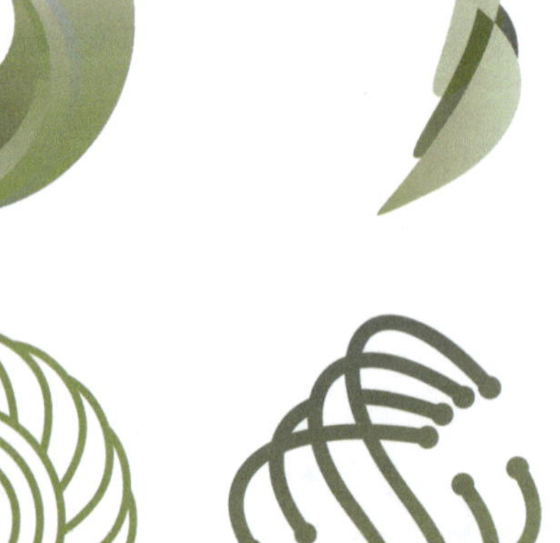

Curved shapes and spirals are typically irregular and provide more freedom and creativity in terms of logo design.

Spirals can evoke a sense of curiosity and healing, which makes them a popular choice for natural products, spas and retreats, and alternative medicine.

SHAPE *Psychology*

Logo shapes can be broken down into three main categories.

SYMBOLIC

Symbolic or abstract logo shapes are some of the most thoughtful and intentionally designed logos. Symbolic logos typically use easily recognizable icons, such as arrows and stars, while abstract logos are often combinations of basic shapes to create a new form that represents an idea or belief.

Abstract logo shapes **CAN SEEM RANDOM,** but are often some of the most thoughtful and intentionally designed forms.

You want your logo to help communicate a story or message, even evoke a feeling, and using abstract shapes can help craft that narrative. These logos tend to grab attention and pique curiosity.

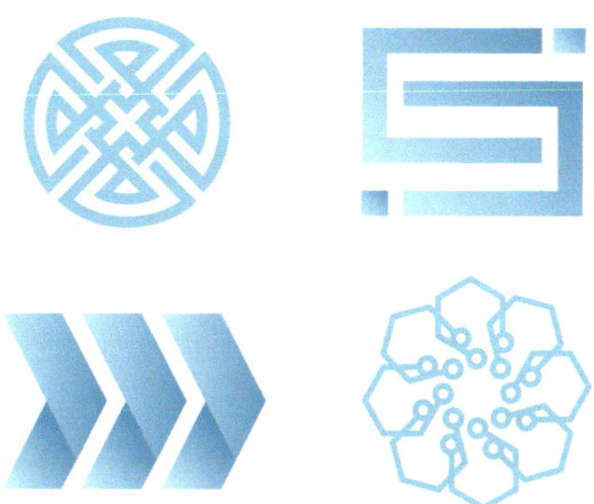

Symbols or cultural shapes include things like hearts, stars, and crosses, which **ALL HAVE A MEANING** that is universally recognized.

It is vital to understand the language and cultural meaning behind specific shapes and the message they communicate, as well as if the message is perceived differently around the world.

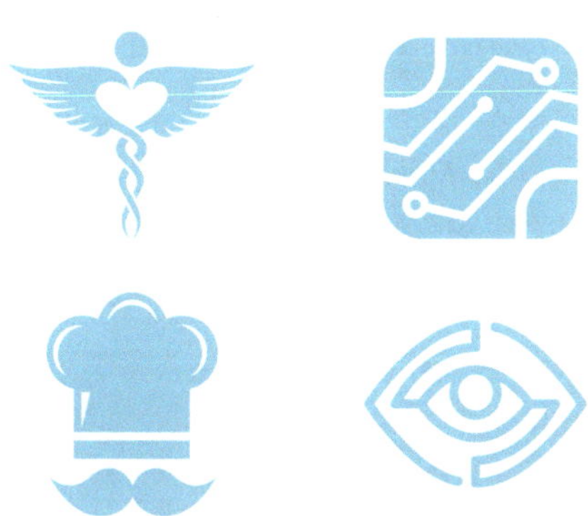

SHAPE *Psychology*

Logo shapes can be broken down into three main categories.

GEOMETRIC

Basic shapes such as circles, triangles, and squares are made up of lines, points, and curves that come together in various combinations. Geometric shapes are structured and tend to be symmetrical.

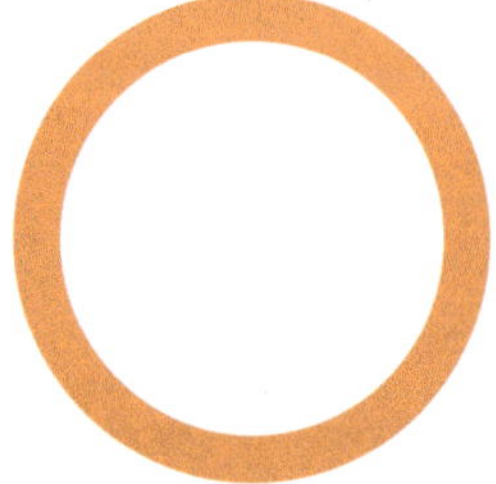

CIRCLES

round and perfect
uniquely non-linear
no sharp edges or corners

symbolizes:
wholeness
perfection
completeness
motion
community
friendship
inclusivity
strength

Clean, simple, and versatile, making them a great choice for any industry.

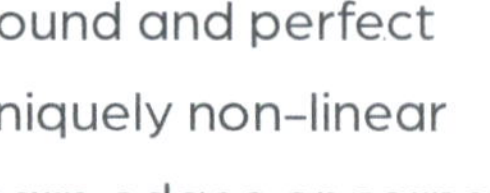

SQUARES & RECTANGLES

symmetrical
balanced
strong

symbolizes:
stability
balance
reliability
strength
professionalism
foundation
firmness

These shapes help anchor the eye and frame the visuals, making it great for many logo projects.

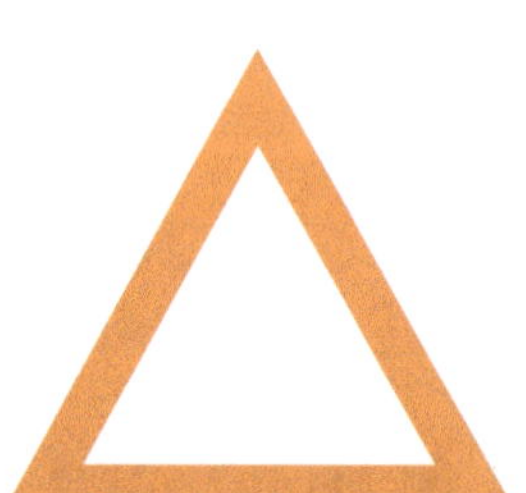

TRIANGLES

definitive corners
multiple edges
indicate direction

symbolizes:
growth
enlighenment
energy
confidence
dependability
trust
strength

Being so flexible and adaptable, triangles make an awesome logo shape.

5 *Questions* to ask yourself to help you choose a logo SHAPE

1 ARE YOU USING THE WHITE SPACE?

While we can't all be the brilliant creator of the arrow in the FedEx logo, we can use it as a reminder to examine the negative or white space in our logo shapes, and see if we are using it effectively.

2 DOES YOUR COLOR MATCH YOUR SHAPE?

The ultimate color of your shape will impact whether it is as effective as you intended, so considering shape and color hand in hand will save you some grief later on. For instance, does a gold star convey the same thing as a green or black star?

3 DOES YOUR FONT AGREE?

It always comes back to the typography. Does your chosen font agree with the shape? Meaning – do they work well together, fit nicely, or even interact effectively?

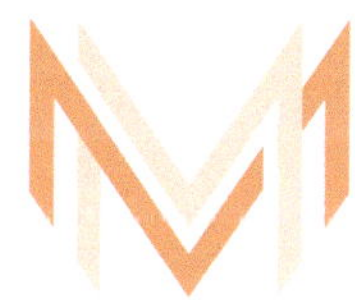

4 WHAT IS YOUR MESSAGE?

What are you trying to say? What industry are you trying to represent with your shape choice? Make sure you walk the line of standing out while also accurately representing the tone and message of what you are trying to communicate.

5 IS THE SHAPE ON BRAND?

Whether you are dealing with an established brand or helping to create the brand identity from scratch, remember that this shape choice should fit in with the overarching vision of the company.

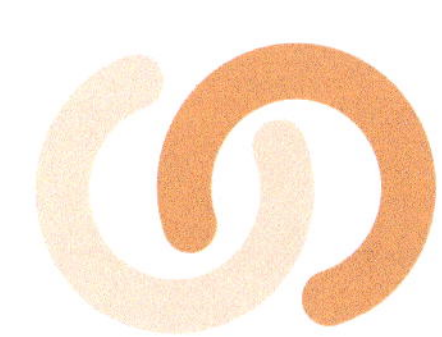

COLOR *Psychology*

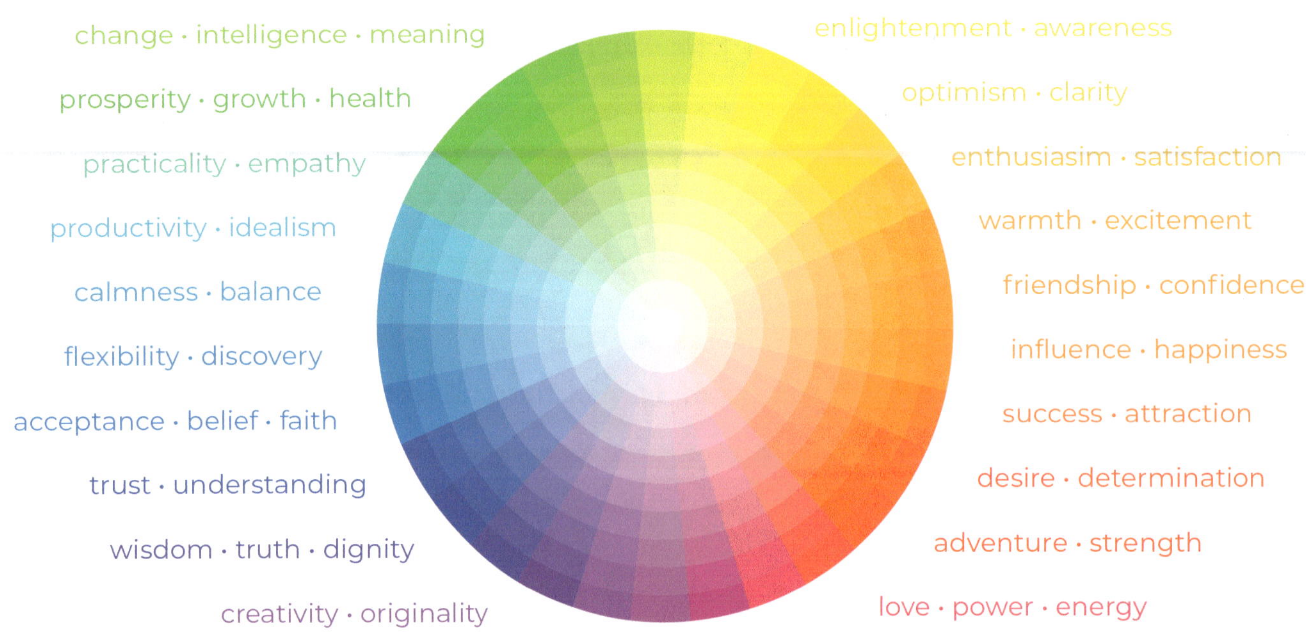

Logo Color Inspiration

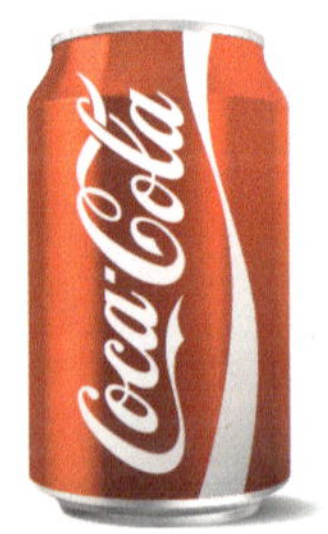

adventure, power, confidence

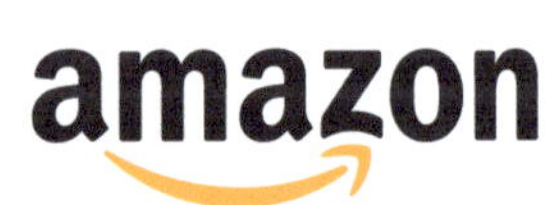

trust, energy, satisfaction

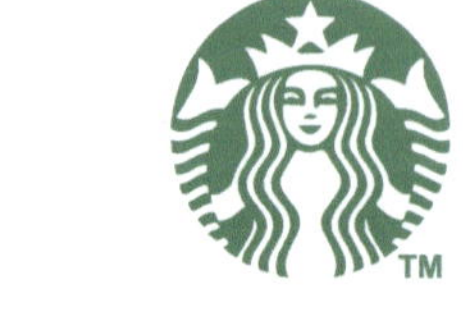
prosperity, growth, health

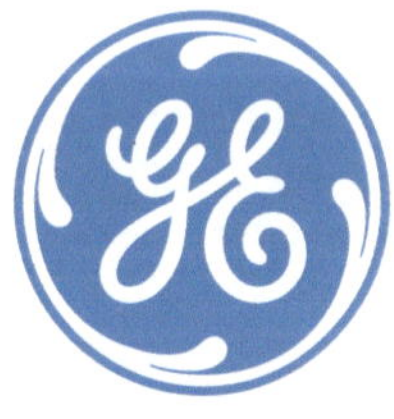
trust, discovery, tranquility

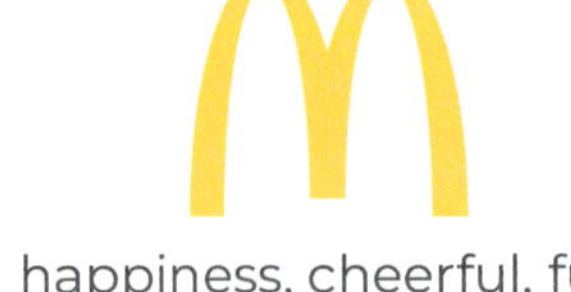
happiness, cheerful, fun

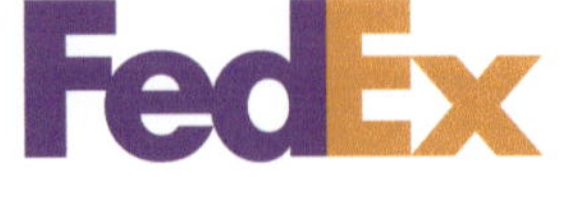

wisdom, creativity, dignity

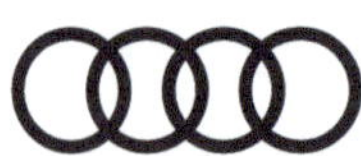
power, modern, strong

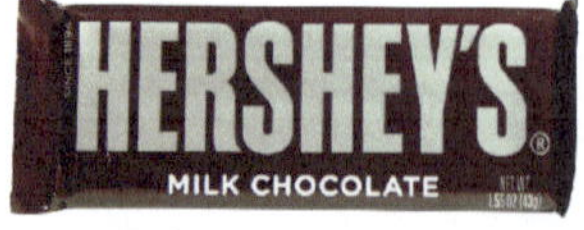

natural, comfortable, friendly

Chapter Five

THE SEVEN TYPES OF LOGOS

Your logo is typically the first element people notice about your brand, so a powerful and strong visual message can highly benefit your company. Let's discuss the seven different types of logo designs, and hopefully understanding them will help guide you in the right direction for your logo project.

The seven different types of logos are:

- abstract
- lettermark
- wordmark
- combination
- emblem
- mascot
- pictorial

Abstract Logos

Abstract logos often don't make much sense at first glance, especially if you don't already know anything about the company. However, they are often very intentional visuals meant to be symbolic of a deeper meaning.

Probably the most widely recognized abstract logo worldwide is the Nike logo. The 'swoosh' shape is synonomous with the Nike brand in a truly impressive way, but if you did not know what the company was, would the 'swoosh' make much sense to you? This is the dilemma with an abstract logo choice. The burden of understanding the message of the logo design is on the audience, and it can be tough to make a successful connection.

While this challenge may not work for all industries or companies, it can be a powerful creative choice in allowing the imagination of your audience to help you convey your intended narrative.

Abstract logos can be especially helpful to a complex company that cannot be contained with one icon or shape. Leaving more up to interpretation can cover a wider range of messaging. However, you should ultimately have a strong message that will help support your abstract logo, establishing an effective brand identity.

If you have not already established some brand recognition, then abstract logos may not be the right choice. If you have some brand identity that is already providing clear messaging, then an abstract logo might be the perfect option to represent an innovative company, without the need to convey literal representations.

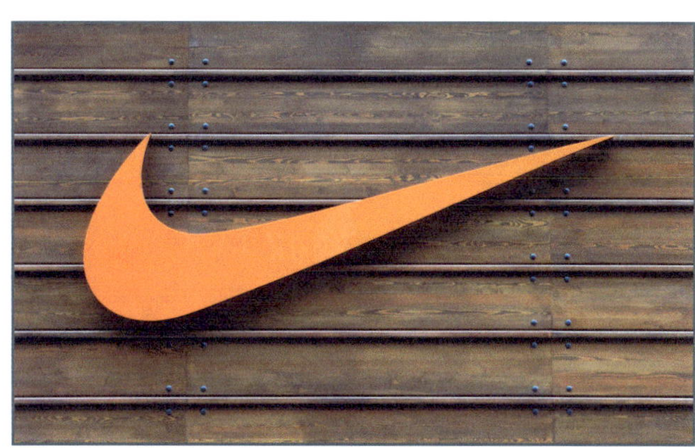

Lettermark Logos

If your company or client has a long business name, then a lettermark or acronym logo could be just the thing you are looking for!

There are many lettermark logos surrounding us every day. Most television networks, for instance, use lettermark logos – CNN, HBO, and ABC for example.

Lettermark logos can be a very straight-forward option that provides a clear and memorable brand identity to help establish a company's identity. Condensing the messaging and making it easily digestible and simple will help your audience to recall it far easier than a lengthy name they might struggle to remember.

If you are designing for a new or fairly unknown company and want to explore a lettermark option, but don't want the full name to be lost, then including the full name as a tagline underneath the lettermark logo can be a good option.

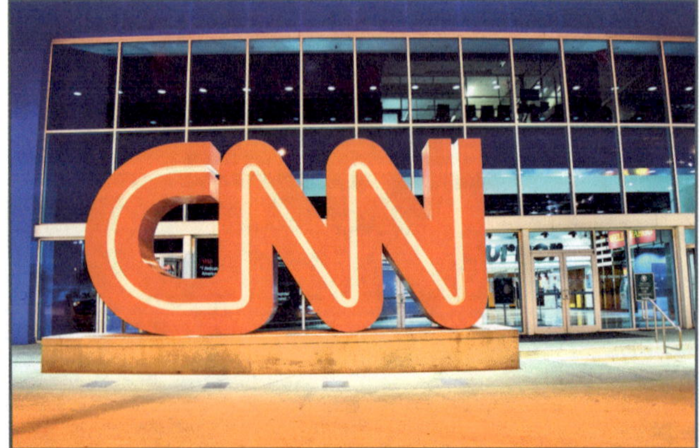

Wordmark Logos

Wordmarks are on the opposite end of the spectrum from abstract logos in that they are only the name of the business. That's it.

It may sound simple, but this logo design approach may be more effective than you think. With no other visual distractions, this logo design can make the name of your business very memorable. Just look at Google. The Google logo is the prime example of a wordmark logo design. It is beautifully simple, bright, easy to read, and, most importantly, memorable.

Isn't the company name what is ultimately the most important thing for your audience to remember? This is what they will be searching for to find you. Wordmark logos can be a perfect choice for small businesses just starting out. However, it is important to remember if you are considering a wordmark logo design that it is all about the typeface. Take your time choosing the right one to represent the business, its characteristics, brand, and so on. Most importantly, though, your wordmark logo should be legible. If your audience can't read it quickly and clearly, then it defeats the entire purpose of a wordmark option.

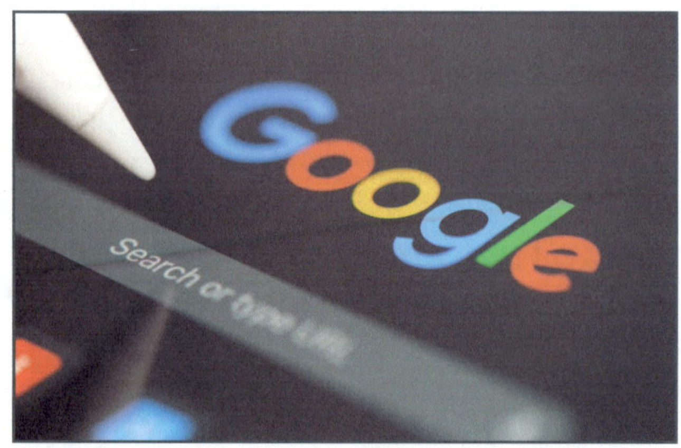

Combination Logos

The combination logo design is probably the most common logo design option chosen—it's a combination of typography (a wordmark or lettermark) and a visual piece such as an icon or image, etc.

The type and visuals work together to represent the company and give context to what the brand is all about. A classic choice that accomplishes several of the other logo design options all in one. While not as simple and recognizable as a wordmark, it has more creative control with the addition of imagery. Similarly, while not as bold and simple as an abstract logo, a combination logo allows for more clarity with the use of text.

Combination logos are often the safest choice and are often recommended for new businesses. Once established, businesses can even choose to utilize their text or imagery individually essentially creating a wordmark or abstract logo from the original. This makes a combination logo a very versatile design option. Dunkin' Donuts is a great example of a company that has a combination logo, but because of its well established brand, it has moved more towards the use of a simple wordmark option.

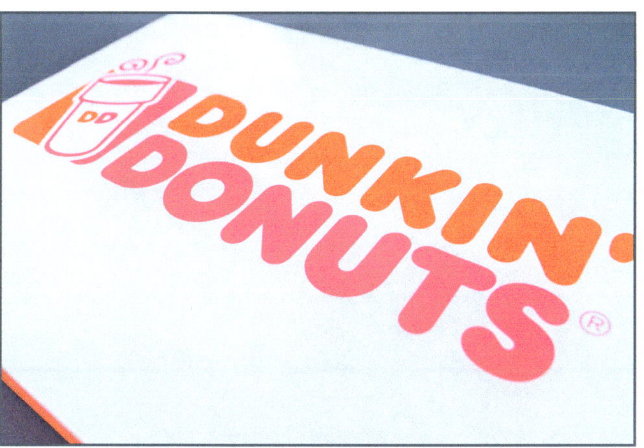

Emblem Logos

Perhaps the oldest type of logos are called emblem logos, which date back to hieroglyphics used by Ancient Egyptians. Many of the oldest internationally recognized logos are emblem logos that may have been modernized over time, but retained their essential design.

Emblem logos are often more formal and complex. A family crest, for instance, would be an emblem logo, and would have many layers and details, all contributing to the ultimate meaning of the design.

Emblem logos can give a sophisticated appearance, suggesting high-end and high-class. Think more traditional and professional, with a detailed story to tell. Due to the intricate nature of an emblem logo, it is highly unlikely you would find a similar logo design in the market.

You really only want to choose an emblem logo approach if you have a ton to communicate and a vast array of iconography to utilize. These logos are not typically easily scalable and do not read well at smaller sizes.

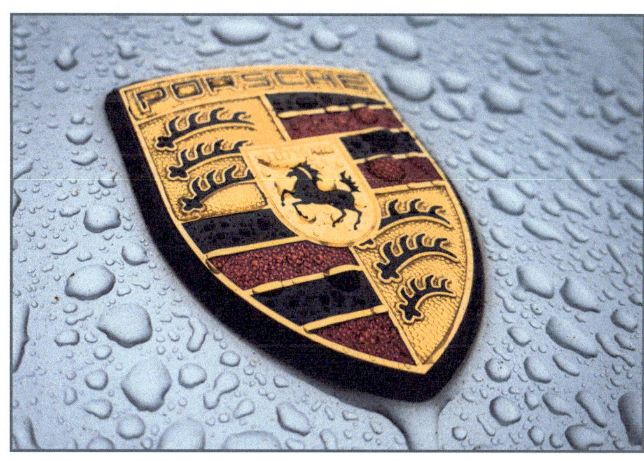

Mascot Logos

A mascot logo is just like it sounds, evoking images of characters dressed up to represent a brand. From the Gecko to the Mouse, to a colonel or a peanut, these are all examples of a mascot logo option. Geico, Disney, KFC, and Planters are just a few examples of the most famous uses of a mascot logo design.

These logos are most popular in industries such as sports, food, and entertainment. Having a mascot logo also gives your business an automatic spokesperson or ambassador, providing your audience something to have an emotional connection to within your brand.

Mascot logos usually have a personal narrative to convey and are able to reach their audience on a deeper level quickly, making them a good option for products and businesses targeted to families or children.

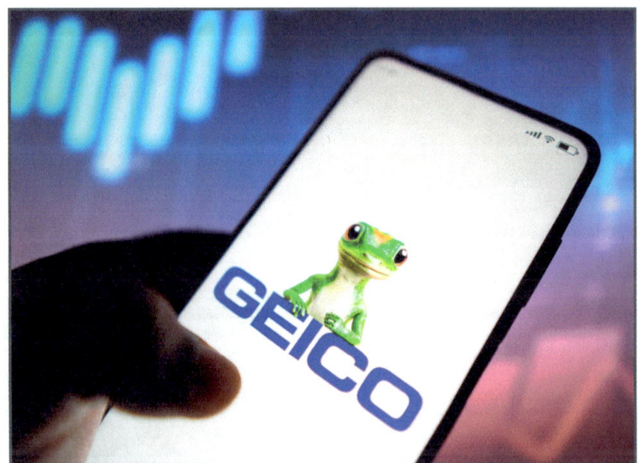

Pictorial Logos

Pictorial logos don't typically tell a story in a direct fashion and are, therefore, not usually an optimal choice for new companies. They are usually created for well established brands as part of a redesign.

They are often visually memorable and creative, and attract the audience that way, but if most people stopped to try to relate the logo design to the brand, they might find that they struggle. For example, Starbucks has a pictorial logo design. Really think about what the Starbucks logo is. Are you surprised to realize it is a mermaid? With two tails? Exactly.

Pictorial and abstract logos share some commonalities in that they rely on the subconscious mind to relate the visuals to the brand. Starbucks chose their design to subconsciously inspire adventure and natural beauty, and they were able to do this because they already had a well established brand.

Creating a successful pictorial logo involves utilizing elements and visuals that your audience relates to and recognizes, but in a new and unique visual approach – not the easiest thing to do.

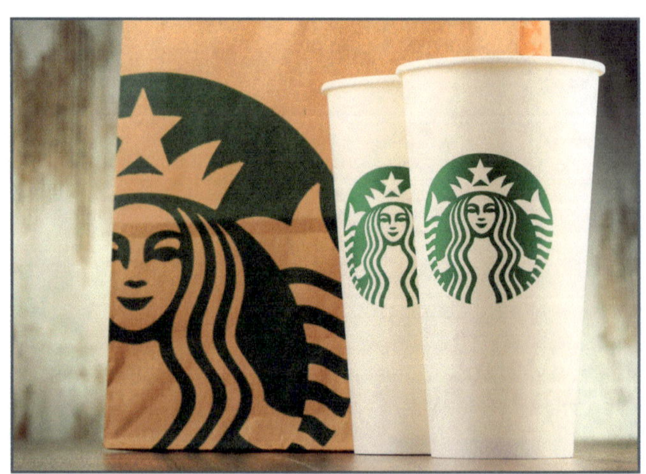

THE 7 TYPES OF LOGO Designs

1 ABSTRACT

Just like it sounds – not obvious, but often intentional visuals meant to be symbolic.

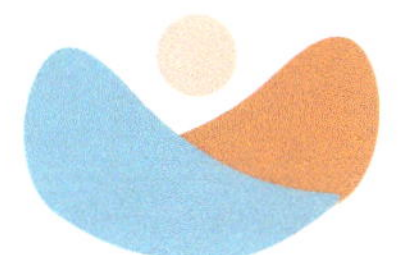
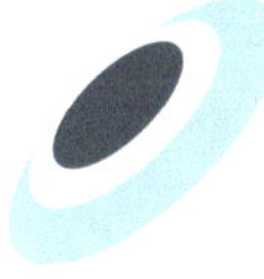

2 LETTERMARK

Usually an acronym of your company name displayed in a stylized fashion.

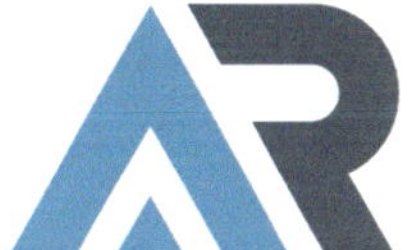
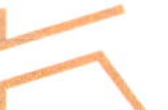
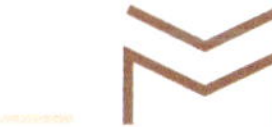

3 WORDMARK

Deceptively simple logo using just the name of the company.

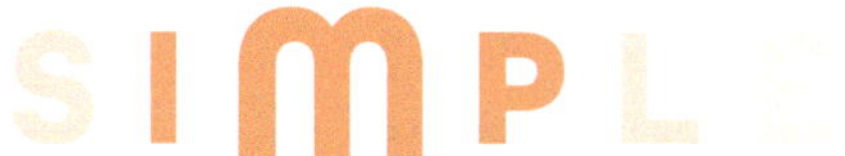

4 COMBINATION

Most common logo design option, combining company name with visuals.

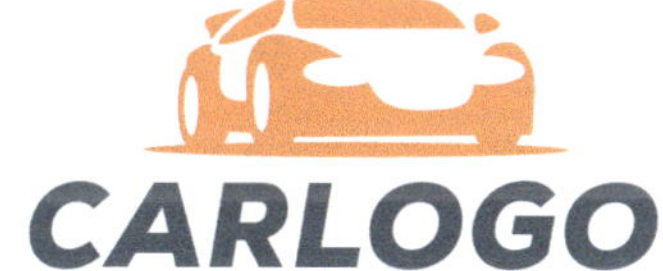

5 EMBLEM

Often complex, sophisticated, or classic logo designs with intricate details.

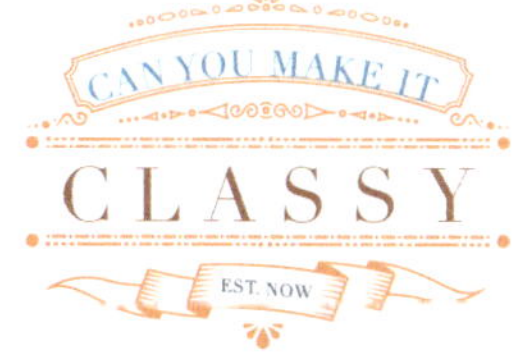

6 MASCOT

Character imagery used to support the logo design for an emotional connection.

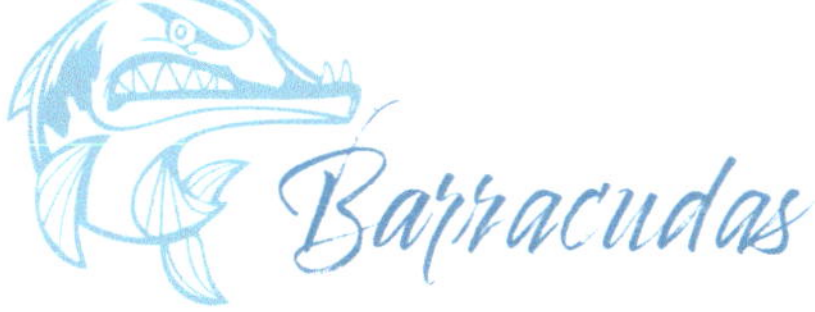

7 PICTORIAL

Usually nonlinear appealing visual that is used with well established companies.

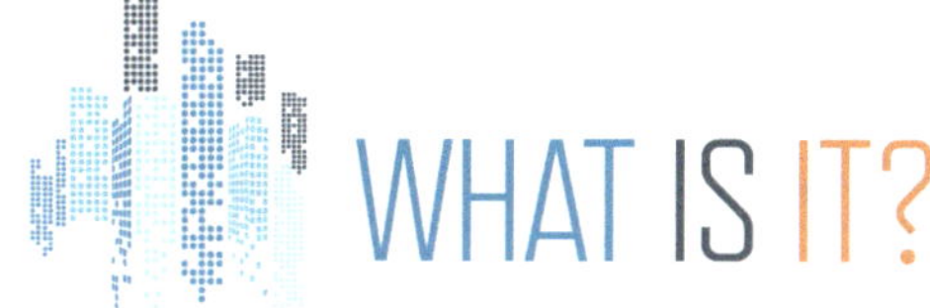

Chapter Six

KNOW THE BRAND & THE COMPETITION

The word research can evoke feelings of anxiety or boredom in many of us, but it can be helpful to slow down and take a minute before jumping in with your logo design.

Logo designs are almost always the first step in a long series of steps in establishing a brand or company. What this also means is that it often provides the foundation upon which that company and brand is built. From colors to typeface, personality, and beyond, the logo design defines many aspects of a company going forward. So it makes sense that all angles should be considered to create a classic, timeless, memorable representation of the company you are creating for.

Research can be a pretty vital part of stepping out on the right foot.

I have told many clients over the years that a logo design is the hardest project to do for a brand. It is typically the only one that starts with a completely blank canvas. Once you have a logo design, all other elements are influenced by that logo design. From iconography to printables, books, websites, and so on, many items will be impacted by the choices made when designing a logo.

So, research can be a pretty vital part of stepping out on the right foot.

Included as a bonus in the back of this book is a helpful questionnaire to send to clients if you are creating for someone else. This helps them to think through some aspects they might not have considered and gives you the first piece of research in your logo design project.

One aspect you want your clients to consider is who their ideal audience is, their target demographic, and what appeals to them. From there, you can look at what is trending for that audience and why.

Another super important part of this step is to know the competition. Who are they? What are they using visually? How do you want to stand out? Understanding what your client likes AND dislikes about their competition's branding can also be incredibly helpful.

Using different colors and styles from your direct competition can be key to ensure your new company doesn't get lost in the mix, but instead remains memorable and different.

Oftentimes a logo client is not someone who considers themselves very creative, so a logo questionnaire can help encourage them to verbalize some elements they might not have thought of. Colors, for example, are obviously very important, and asking them to think about what colors appeal to them and especially what colors do not appeal to them can help you in your design choices.

Asking them to consider what words describe their brand, and ultimately their logo, can also be quite enlightening. If they can describe what emotional response they want their audience to ideally have, that is also an aspect to help provide clarity for your design choices.

The trick is to follow your client's lead when it makes sense and helping to lead them when that makes more sense.

The questionnaire also asks them to consider what slogan, if any, they are planning to use. This simple line can actually be quite useful for design ideas, especially imagery. It is also important to know how often your client plans to use this slogan with their final logo design.

I find that this questionnaire gives you a great base for additional questions and research-if you still feel like you need more.

Typically at this point, I jump in.

I have been known to say to my clients that I find it is important to start to have something to look at and react to. Being a very visual person, I like to start to get visual ideas going pretty early on. I believe I find out a ton of useful information about where to go with a logo design based on my client's reaction to the initial design ideas. Sometimes a client reacts strongly to a color, whether postively or negatively, which is helpful in narrowing down the design direction. Similarly, reactions to a typeface can be very insightful to understand what they are looking for.

There is no right answer for how much research is necessary for your logo design project, and it will vary greatly if it is anything like the hundreds of logo design projects I have done. The trick is to follow your client's lead when it makes sense and helping to lead them when that makes more sense.

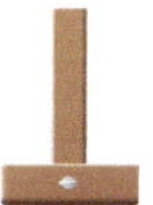

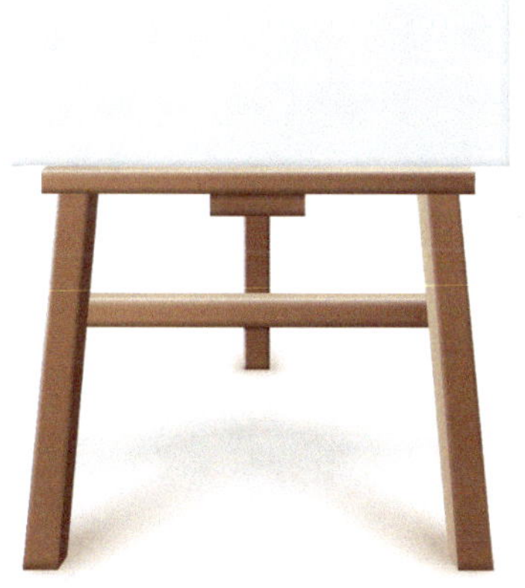

Chapter Seven

10 STEPS TO YOUR NEXT GREAT LOGO

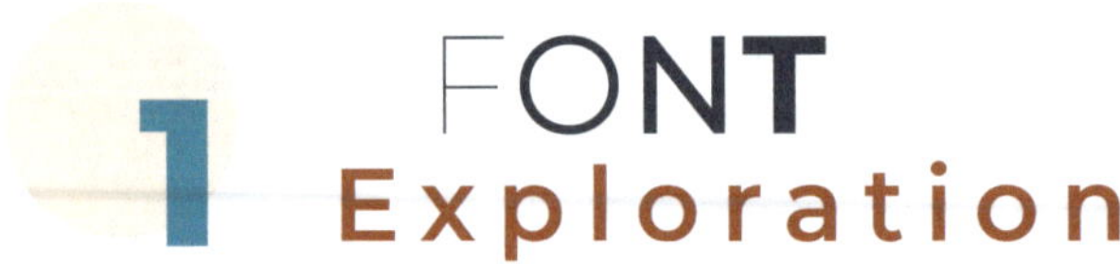

One of the first things I like to do with a logo project is going on a typeface deep dive. I comb through font families and try out the company name in a ton of them to see what strikes me. I call it the "font exploration" part of the process.

Refer back to the what different font families can mean to help you explore the styles that make sense for your brand. Play around with upper and lowercase, kerning and leading, and bold and italic as well.

2 Use your space *effectively.*

Using the space effectively does not necessarily mean to fill it up. Knowing when and how to utilize white space in a logo design can be key.

Experiment with different layout options as you design your initial concepts. Try breaking up the text into two lines for instance, or increase the breathing room between the text and imagery, or shrink it. Moving things around and playing with placement will help you to explore options you might not have thought of.

COMPANY

COMPANY

COMPANY

Company

COMPANY

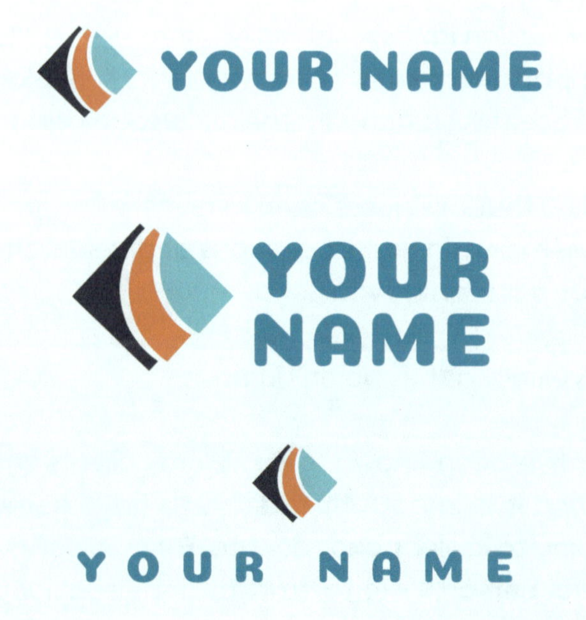

3 To tagline or not to tagline.

If your logo has a tagline, it is always a good idea to have an option with and without the tagline for versaility. A simple rule to remember is to make your tagline shorter than your company name. This may involve shrinking the size of the tagline or using a different font, as well as keeping the tagline succinct.

It is also a good rule to make your tagline font thinner and simpler than your company name font. It is also important that your tagline is aligned with your company name, whether centered or justified to one side, creating a visual balance.

4 Can you READ IT?

This seems like an obvious one, but look around, and I bet you will find some examples of logos that do not accomplish this basic rule. This can happen when you choose a font that is too hard to read for example, or my biggest pet peeve, using all capital letters in a script font. Putting icons or imagery too close to or on top of the text can also cause readability issues.

In order for your logo design to be effective, it has to be able to be read by your audience, so ensuring its readability is definitely vital to the ultimate effectiveness of your design.

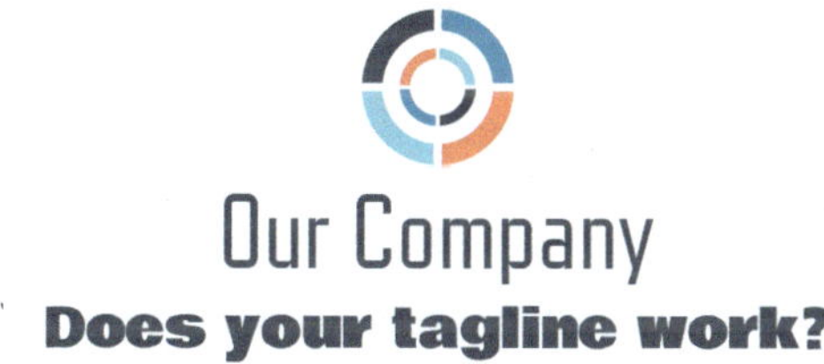

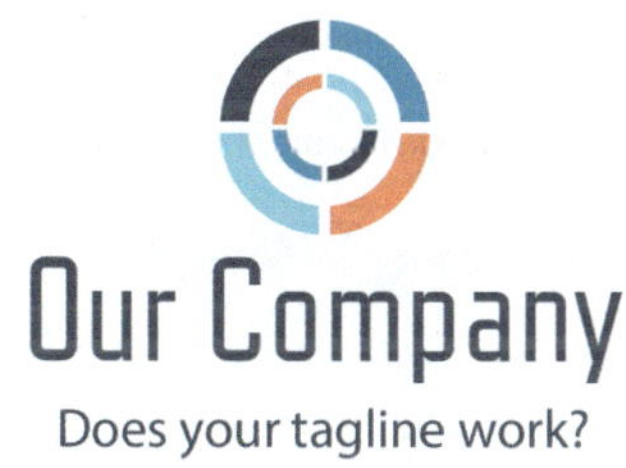

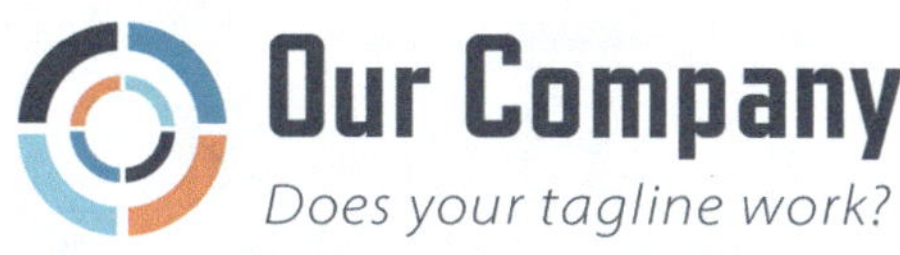

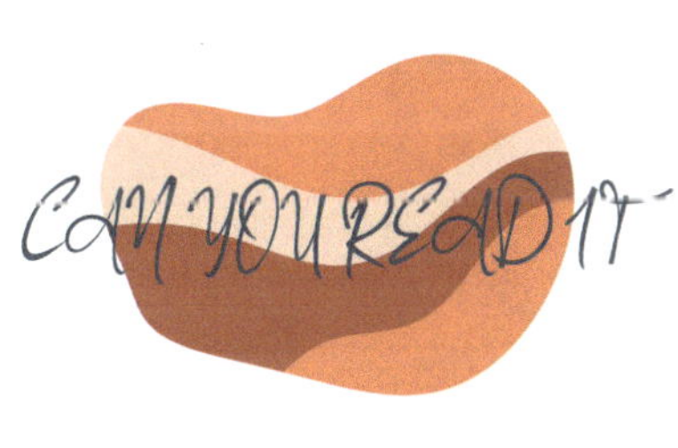

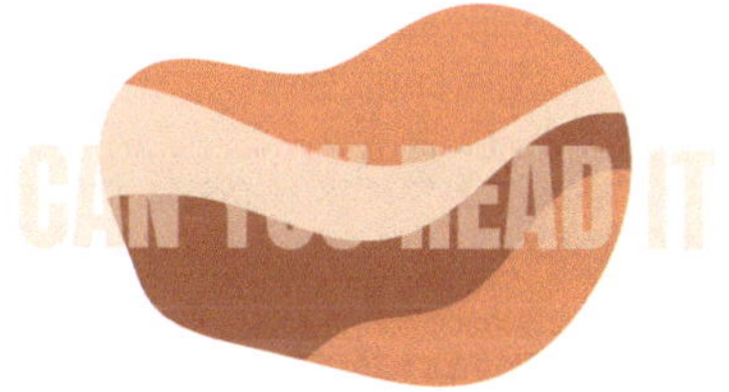

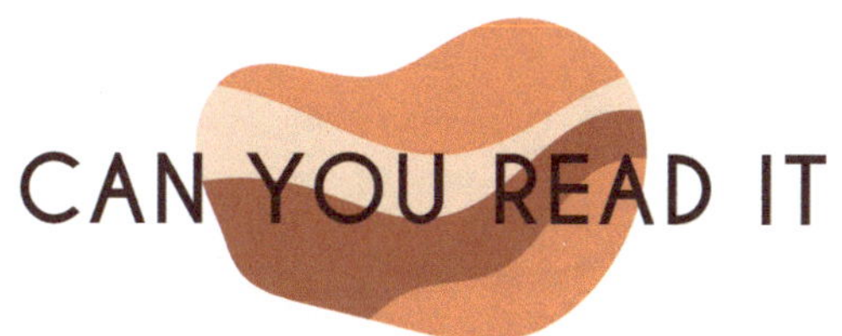

5 Does it sCALE?

Along the same line as the readability of your logo design is the concept of scaling. Make sure your design looks good and is legible at a variety of sizes. Whether it is on a billboard or a sticker, your logo should be clear. Check your logo design at various sizes to ensure it is still legible.

Big or small, your logo should always be recognizable to your audience. Logos that are too detailed or intricate can be challenging to scale down. There is no perfect size for logos, but definitely make sure your logo is a vector file that can be easily scaled without losing resolution.

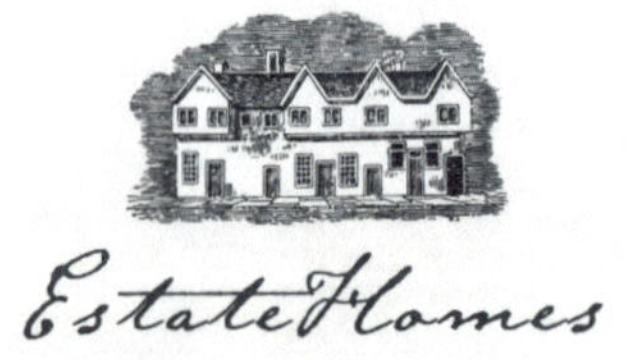

EstateHomes

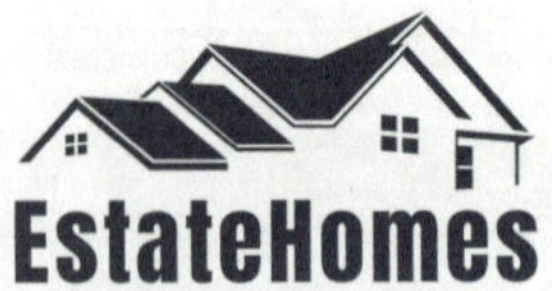

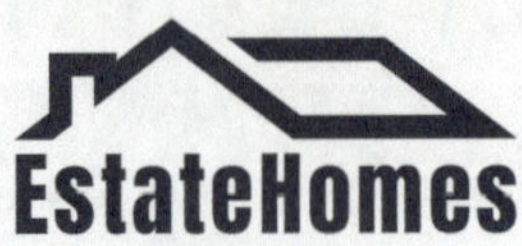

6 Let it breathe. Alignment is key.

From white space to framing, these logo design decisions are important to consider, and even more important is making sure your design has breathing room. If you choose to use a frame element in your logo, whether a box or other shape, leave enough space around your other elements to create white space.

How you choose to align your logo is also something important to consider. Are you going to center all of the elements, or are they left justified, or is the icon is to the left of text or the right? Decisions, decisions. Experiment with different options.

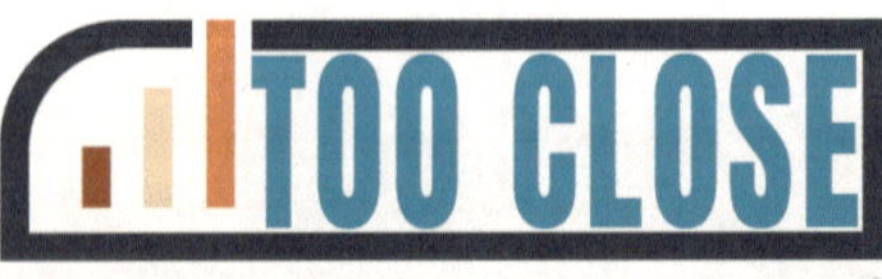

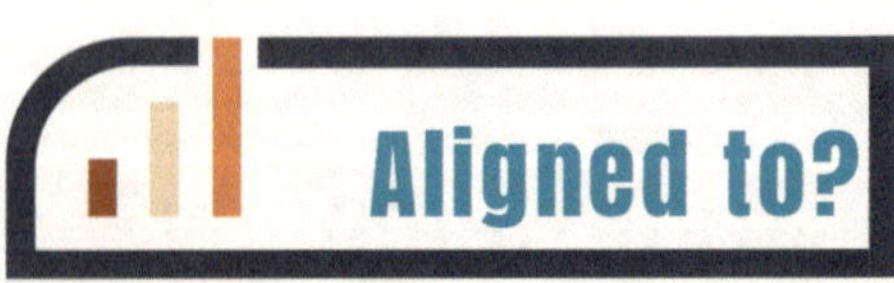

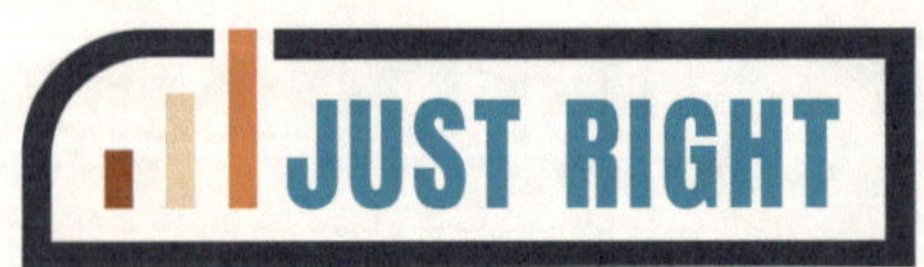

7 Is there an ICON?

A common misconception is that any iconography in a logo design has to be literal, representing exactly what your industry is. This may be the direction you decide to go, but there is also the abstract logo option to consider. It might help to approach your logo icon as a symbol rather than an image.

It should also be easily recognizable and quickly memorable in order to be super effective. The size of your icon impacts the placement of other elements of your logo design and in general shouldn't be smaller than the text portion.

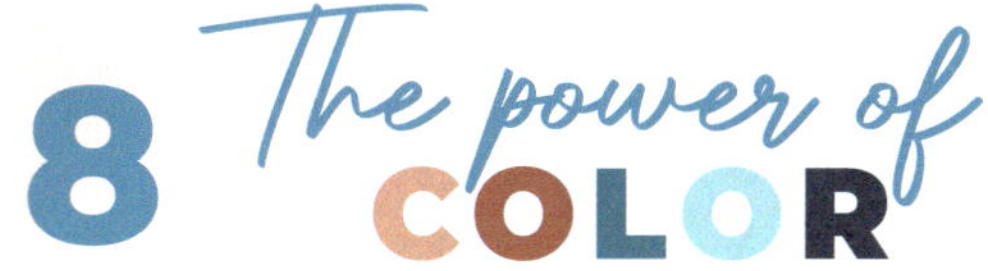

At a certain point, you want to start experimenting with adding color to your designs. Refer back to the color wheel and see what each color family can convey in terms of emotions. Think about the brand you are designing for and use the wheel to get inspired by the different color options to evoke the emotion you are aiming for.

Once a logo design is narrowed down, I do a color exploration with my clients to try several different color combinations or individual colors in order to achieve the visual messaging they are hoping for.

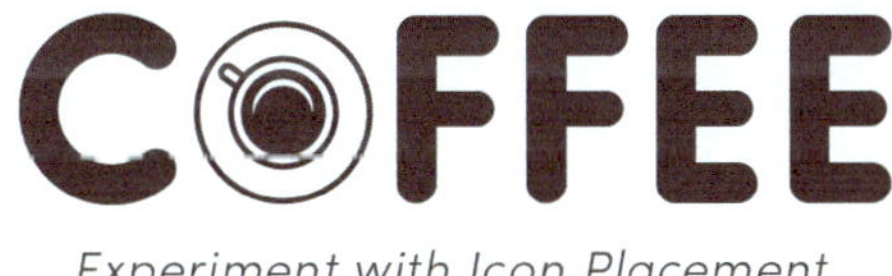

Experiment with Icon Placement

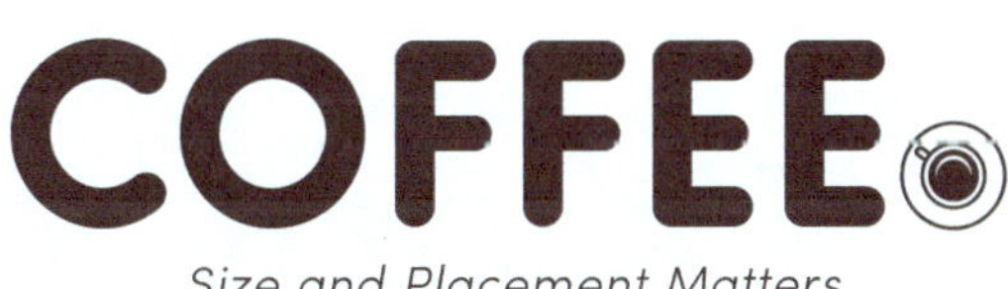

Size and Placement Matters

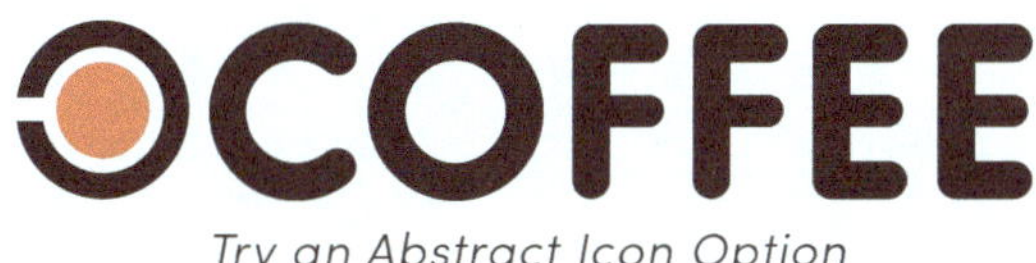

Try an Abstract Icon Option

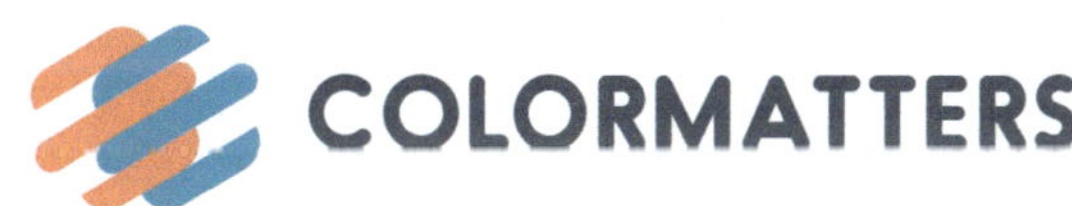

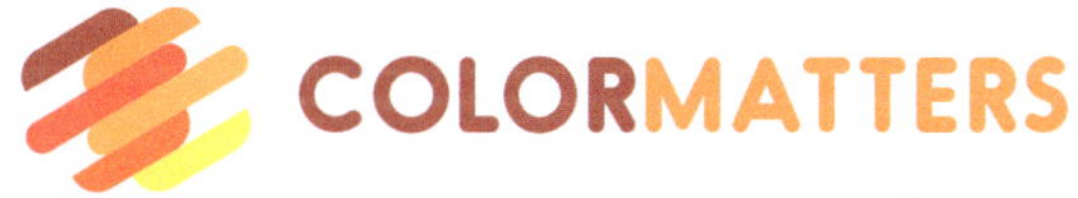

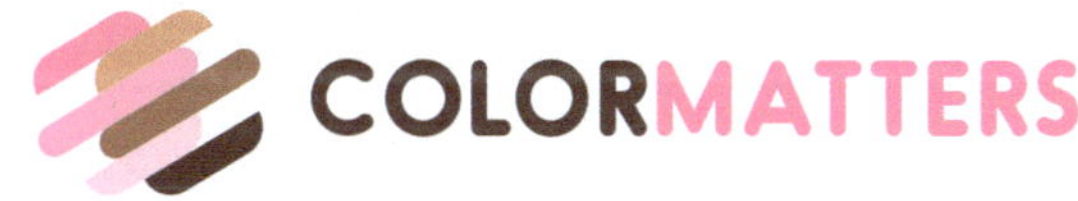

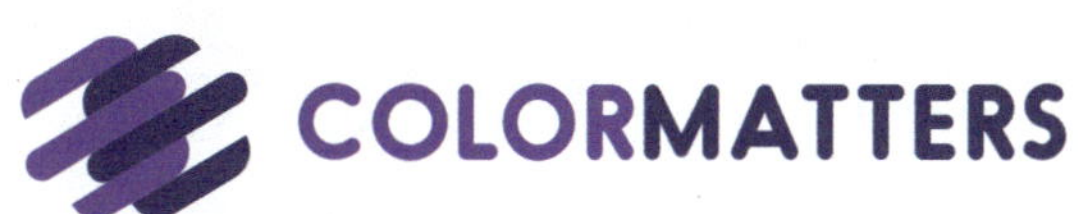

9 Compare & CONTRAST.

Another thing to consider is whether your logo is going to be used predominatly on a white background or a dark background or maybe what it would look like on both. If your logo design will have a background color, be sure to keep the legibility of the design in mind and create enough contrast between the elements.

Similarly, If your logo will have white elements, make sure that the color behind those elements is dark enough to make them effectively visible.

10 Keep it classic & unforgettable.

While following trends can be enticing, be sure to create a classic foundation for your logo design that can hopefully grow and adapt to changing times without losing its core visual.

As I mentioned, your logo design is the first step in creating everything else that goes in to your brand, so take the time to make it right the first time.

Lastly, the most important thing is to make it memorable. An unforgettable logo design is not an easy task to accomplish, but it should be the ultimate goal and should play a part in the choices you make as you create your logo design.

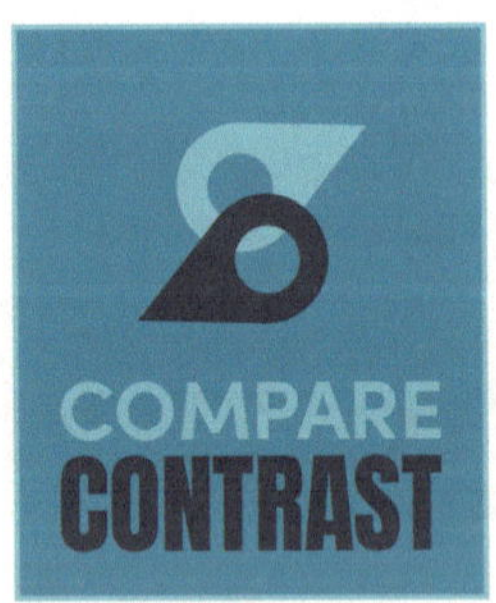

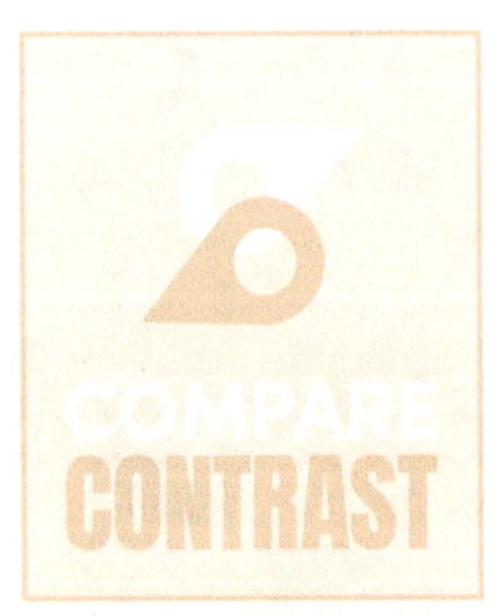

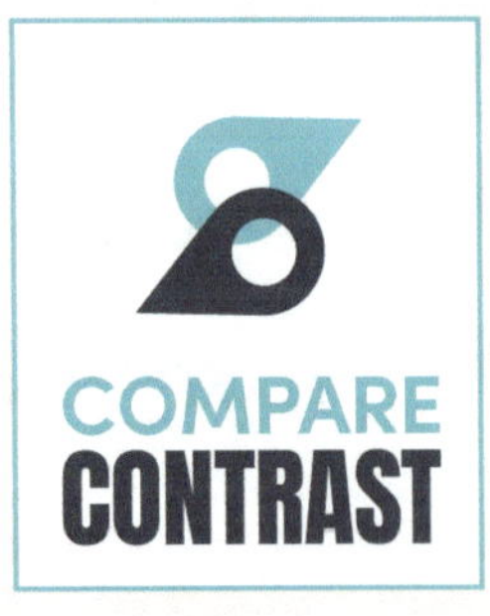

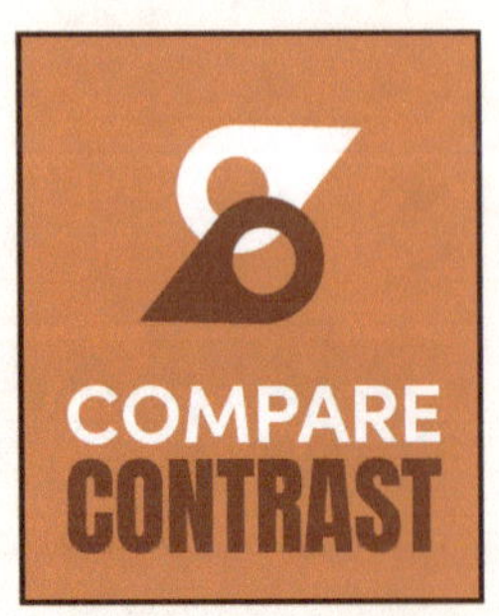

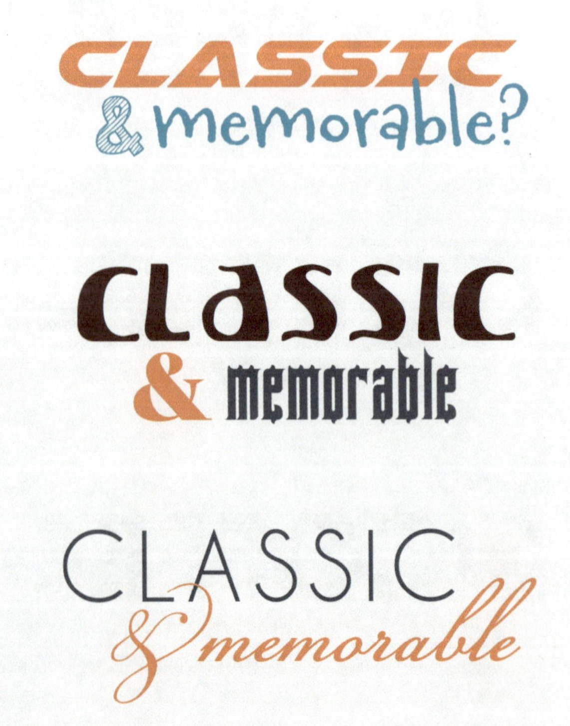

10 STEPS TO YOUR NEXT GREAT LOGO *Design*

1 FONT Exploration

TIP: Play around with upper and lowercase, kerning and leading, and bold and italic as well.

6 Let it breathe. Alignment is key.

TIP: Balance is key. Keep things balanced and not too close to other elements/edges.

2 Use your space *effectively.*

TIP: Experiment with layout and how to utilize white space in your logo design.

7 Is there an ICON?

TIP: Experiment with literal and abstract imagery, as well as no imagery.

3 *To tagline or* not to tagline.

TIP: In general, a tagline should be shorter and thinner than the main logo text.

8 *The power of* COLOR

TIP: Reference the color wheel for each color's emotional response.

4 Can you READ IT?

TIP: Choose a font and color combination that keeps every element legible.

9 Compare & CONTRAST.

TIP: Making sure the important elements of your logo are clear and legible is vital.

5 Does it sCALE?

TIP: Always create logos in vector format, giving you the most scalability without loss.

10 *Keep it classic* & unforgettable.

TIP: Don't get lost in trends so much that you forget that timelessness is the goal.

Chapter Eight

10 COMMON LOGO MiSTAKES TO AVOiD

A logo design is a very important part of a company's branding, and it is important to start off on the right foot. Take your time and try to avoid these common mistakes.

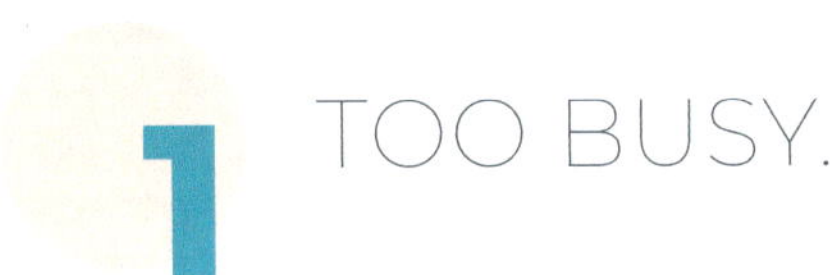

1 TOO BUSY.

It can be tempting to go overboard and throw everything but the kitchen sink into your logo to try to illustrate everything about your company. Resist! Simplicity is the key to a balanced logo design. This does not mean boring, but rather more intentional in the included logo elements.

Don't forget about scalability, so keeping that in mind should help you remember to make your logo design versatile for many uses. Your logo design should be clear to the audience as soon as they look at it. That doesn't necessarily mean they grasp every meaning or intention, but they shouldn't be confused by what they are looking at.

Making it memorable is also the ultimate goal, right? So, keeping your logo design from becoming too busy will help the audience remember it more easily. Remember rule #1 - K.I.S.S.: Keep it simple stupid.

2 TOO MANY FONTS.

The right typeface and the right combination of typefaces can completely define a successful logo design. Similarly to mistake #1, adding in too many fonts or fonts that are too intricate and complicated to your logo design could ruin it.

Go on your font exploration thoroughly, but don't get overexcited about fonts and let them take over your design. Be selective in your font choices and refer back to the font psychology lists to help.

3 TOO BORING.

Keep the first two mistakes in mind, but don't let them scare you away from being interesting! While a logo like Google's is simple in it's design, this does not make it boring. It is a fine line to walk when opting to go with a more basic approach, without imagery for instance.

Achieving successful simplicity in a logo design is no easy feat. Balance, balance, balance.

4 TOO ABSTRACT.

Along the same lines as being too boring is being too abstract and losing your ultimate meaning or message. The last thing you want is for the audience to be confused about your logo design. The goal should be a design that is simple but does not lose its intended communication.

Simple details make all the difference between a random design with no meaning and a thoughtful design that conveys your company's personality through color, font choice, icons, and layout.

5 TOO LITERAL.

The idea is to find a happy medium between too abstract and too literal. While using a coffee cup in a coffee shop logo is not necessarily a bad thing, trying to be more creative and unique in how it is represented should serve to help your company stand out among the masses.

Experiment with different levels of realism when incorporating an everyday object in your logo design. If you are designing for a client, it is often a good idea to give them a variety of options, as you never know which way they are going to lean.

6 TOO SIMILAR.

While it is important to know your competition, it is equally important not to mimic them. You want your company to stand out, not blend in, and definitely not look like a copycat design.

This is also illegal and a copyright violation, so should truly be avoided at all costs.

You want your design to be uniquely yours, and while being inspired by logo designs around you, make sure you are using your own creativity to produce a one-of-a-kind design.

7 TOO TRENDY.

Remember the rule about keeping your logo design classic and timeless. This is hard to do if you get drawn in by the latest trends in design and let them takeover. This does not mean to ignore what is modern and current, but to combine them carefully with classic design principles.

You want your logo design to stand the test of time. While many logos are updated over the years, the most successful ones are those that are able to keep their core visual in place throughout all the latest trends.

8 TOO MANY COLORS.

Another element of your logo design that needs balance are the color choices. Keeping your logo's coloring in line with the personality you are trying to convey is key. Overloading your logo with color can contribute to confusion which is the opposite of what you are trying to achieve.

Typically, when starting a logo design, you want to leave color out of it completely. This is not always the case, but it can be very helpful to focus on just the design elements and the font before playing with colors.

9 TOO UNCLEAR.

Your logo design is ultimately all about messaging. Sometimes logos are more literal, and sometimes they are more abstract, but successful logos always have an underlying thing in common - effective communication.

Your logo's font, color, and imagery choices provide your audience insight into the personality, emotional connection, and intended purpose of your company. You should try to ensure that your message is simple and clear, especially with brands that are not yet established.

10 NOT VECTOR.

This might be the golden rule, and one I learned very early on, when I designed a logo that was not vector. A rasterized image is the last thing you want for a logo design. It will limit you in ways you don't even realize.

A vector file is vital to a logo design so that it can be utilized across all platforms and sizes. Vector files scale without losing any detail and are clear at any size. Raster image files with look blurry if the are sized beyond their original dimensions.

I cannot stress this mistake enough - avoid raster images and always create logo designs in a vector format.

Now that you are equipped with all of these quick reference lists to refer back to as you work on your logo design, let's review and see if your logo design is done!

COMMON *Logo Design* MISTAKES TO AVOID

1 TOO BUSY.

TIP: Resist the temptation to throw every-thing in your logo. Simplicity is key.

2 TOO MANY FONTS.

TIP: Explore as many fonts as you like, but when you make your final choices, keep it to 2 max.

3 TOO BORING.

TIP: Simple doesn't mean boring. Walk the line between too much and too little.

4 TOO ABSTRACT.

TIP: Confusion is a killer of a logo's purpose. Don't create a puzzle for your audience.

5 TOO LITERAL.

TIP: Experiment with imagery to get varying degrees of realism and representation.

6 TOO SIMILAR.

TIP: Don't copy other logos. Be inspired, but be careful to keep your work original.

7 TOO TRENDY.

TIP: Try not to get sucked in by trends and lose your goal of a classic, timeless appeal.

8 TOO MANY COLORS.

TIP: While color is key, don't let it take over and go off the rails into a big mess.

9 TOO UNCLEAR.

TIP: Keep your message clear. Always come back to simple and balanced.

10 NOT VECTOR.

TIP: Just keep it vector, right from the start. It will save you so many headaches.

Chapter Nine

QUESTIONS TO ASK YOURSELF - iS YOUR LOGO DONE?

Now that your logo design is complete, you should ask yourself these questions to ensure you are ready to send it off to the client or use it yourself. As you design more and more logos, these questions should become unnecessary and just part of your process.

Is my logo scalable?

This goes back to creating your logo in a vector format from the very beginning. That way you are never limited in the scalability of your design, and can go as large as a billboard or as small as a sticker without losing any quality! Once you have a vector file from the start, you can create any format your heart, or a printer, desires, from a PDF to a JPG, and so on.

You should also check your design at various sizes to make sure it is still legible when very small or very large. Consider the various places your logo could go and how it would look.

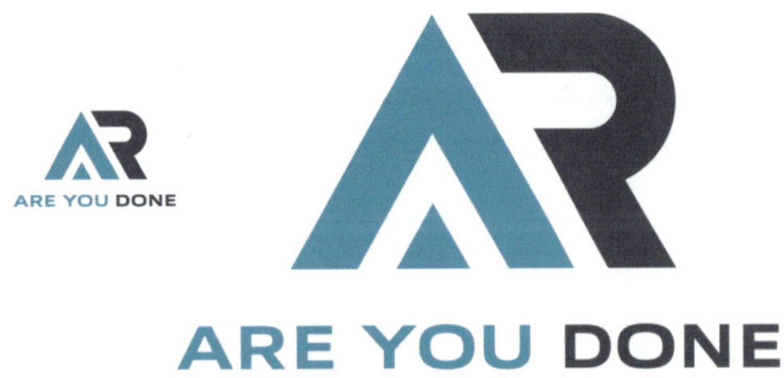

Where will I be using my logo design the most and does it look its best there?

Will it be online or in print? Will it primarily be large or small? Check your logo design in the applications that you intend to use it in the most, and verify that it is good to go.

If it is on social media, check the latest optimal sizes for the various platforms, and see if any tweaking is necessary to optimize your logo design.

If it is in print, then definitely try doing just that - printing it! Whether you want to have it printed professionally, or just want to print out a test on your own printer, at least see it off the screen to see if you notice anything that could be improved.

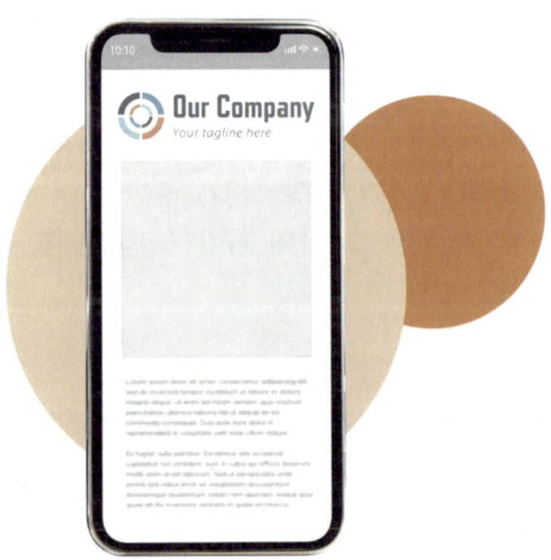

Is the logo design optimized for color AND black and white?

It is always a good idea to have a basic black and white version of a logo design for anytime that color may not be an option. Even a grayscale version might prove worthwhile. A one color logo option is often useful as well to potentially save costs on printing or for embroidery.

It is a good idea to include options in your final deliverables to clients or for your own logo designs. You never know when it can come in handy.

You can always adjust the logo design slightly to make it ideal for a black and white version. For example, you might have to simplify some lines or outline a larger colorful item to make it read correctly in just black and white.

Creating these various options from the beginning will save you headaches down the road!

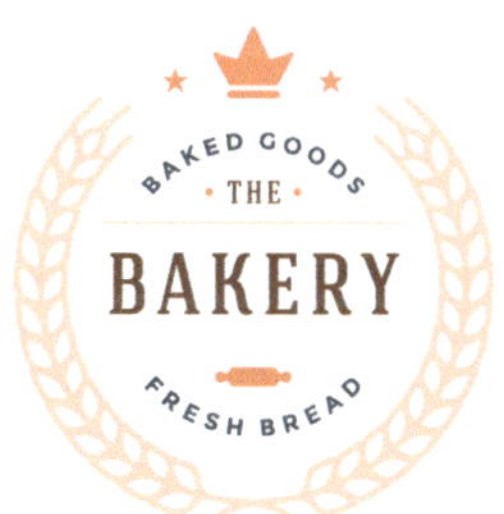

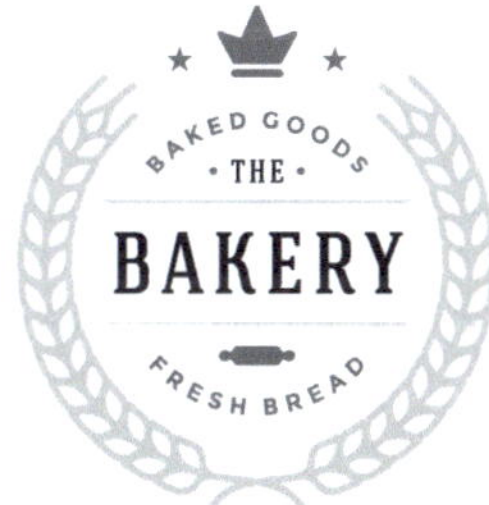

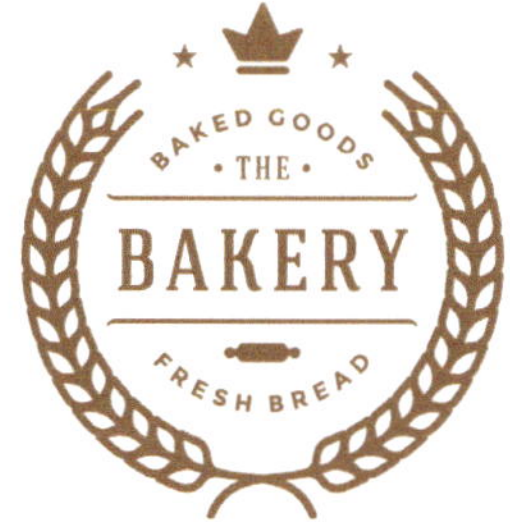

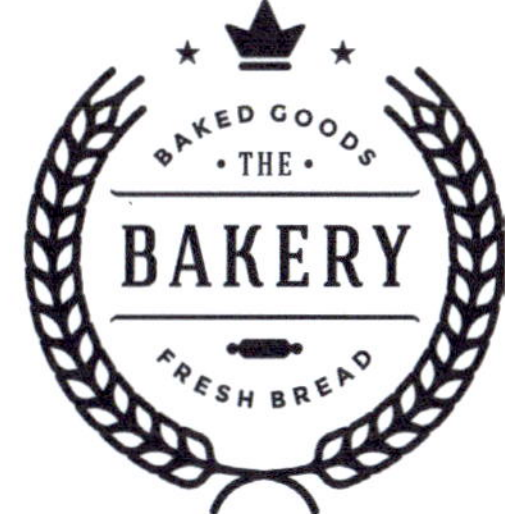

Do I have various formatting options?

Along that same line of thinking is to make sure you have created options for your logo design. Often a horizontal and vertical option can be helpful, as you will find there are instances where different formats allow for better readability.

If you have both text and a visual, then consider creating options with just text and options with just the visual - how does that look? Does it still work for your brand? If not, then ensure your style guide explains that they shouldn't be used independently.

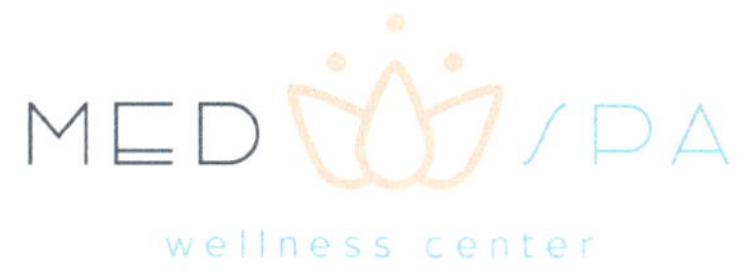

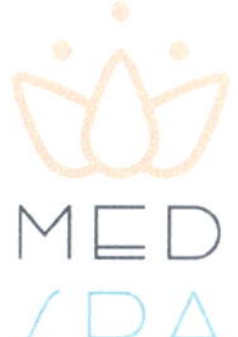

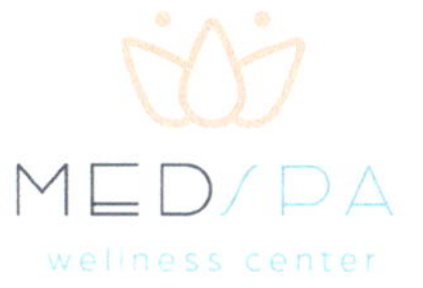

Done!

Now that you are really truly done, it is time to create a style guide. This is where you establish the logo usage guidelines and how your logo design should be optimally utilized.

For smaller projects, this step might not be necessary, but for clients, whether a small or large business, it is a nice professional touch that will truly complete your logo design project. The next chapter will walk through how to create a quick and beautiful style guide.

Chapter Ten

CREATING A STYLE GUiDE

Let's start with how to create a simple, clear, and professional one page style guide. We will touch on how to create a complete brand guideline for a business, but mostly we are going to focus on an intial straightforward option to get you started. A one page style guide can contain the essentials and can always be used to grow as a business grows, and more rules and guidelines are necessary.

Below is an example of a one page style guide that contains all of the brand essentials to get you started, and then we will break it down on the next page.

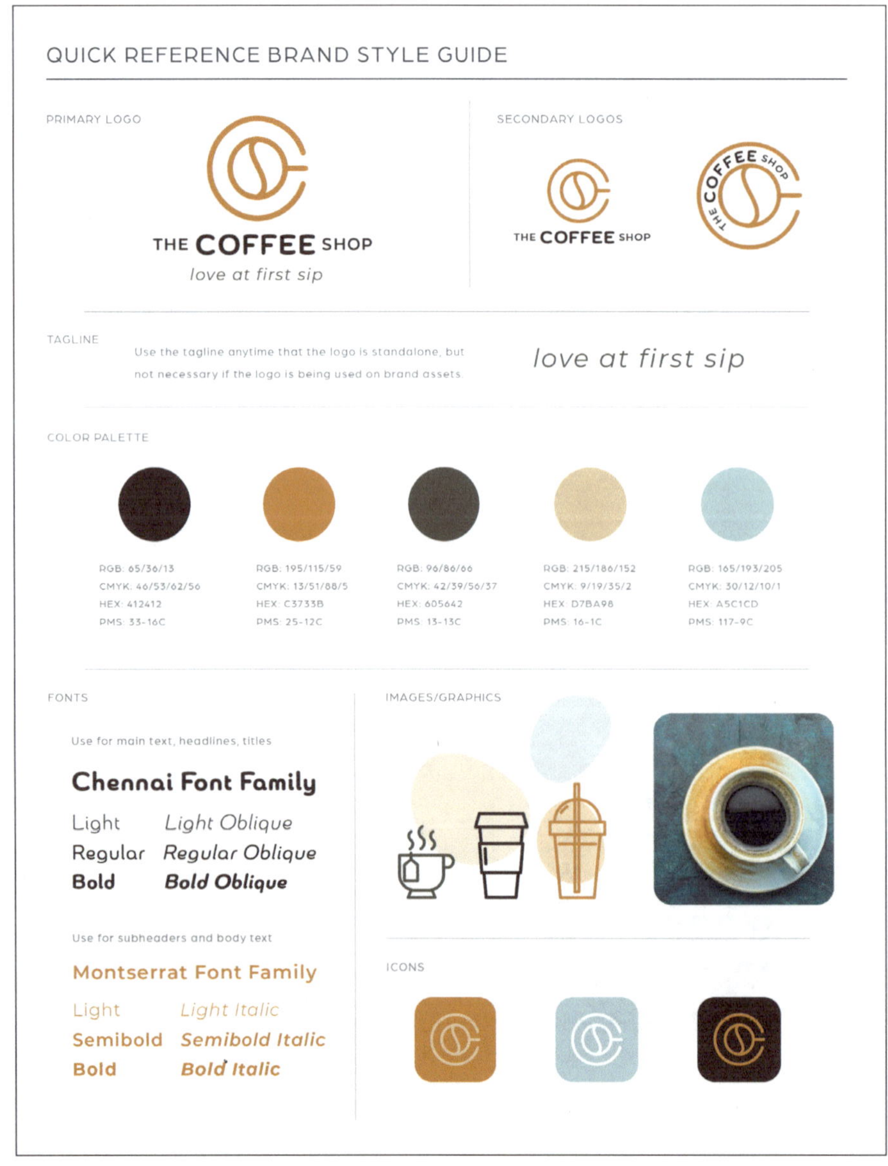

Logo

The first item you will want to include in your logo style guide is, in fact, the logo design. You will want to show the main primary logo design, as well as any alternate design options, and a brief explanation of when to use each.

The purpose of this information is to literally guide anyone who is using the logo in the best practices that you have set forth to achieve optimal results. Include the optimal size and proportions of the logo, as well as the preferred white space around the design.

PRIMARY LOGO

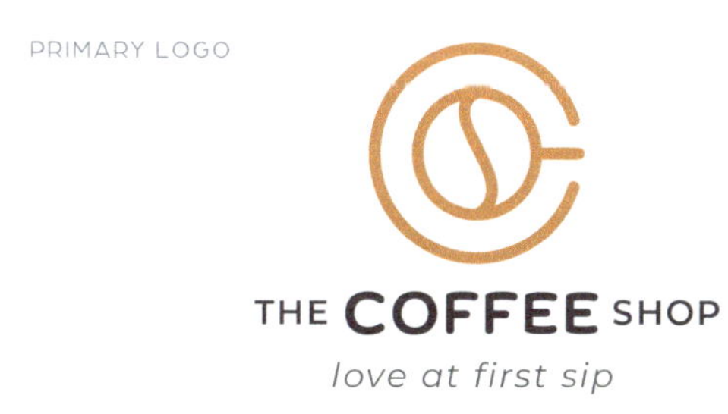

SECONDARY LOGOS

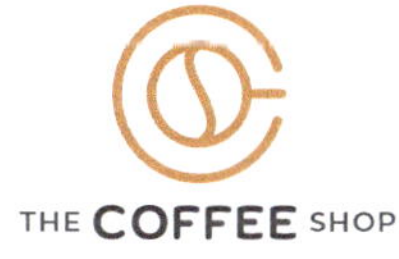

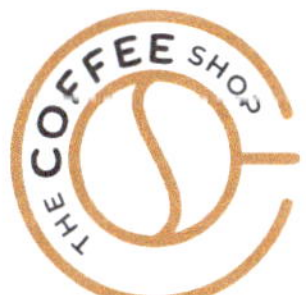

Colors

Your color palette should be as consistent as your logo design itself. The colors you use should become associated with your brand, as well as your logo design. Consistent use of the color palette will help to achieve this.

It is also helpful to include color codes, such as RGB and HEX (for web use), CMYK (for print use), and PMS (for color matching for print). Include any secondary or supporting colors, but ideally your color palette should be 3–5 colors.

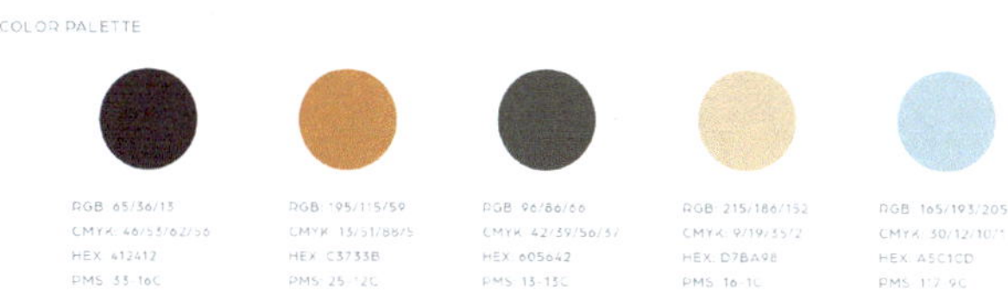

Fonts

You should include a list of the fonts included in your logo as well as the ideal secondary font (if any) for supporting text. Font famliies with several options in the form of light, bold, and italics are ideal as they allow for more options while maintaining consistency.

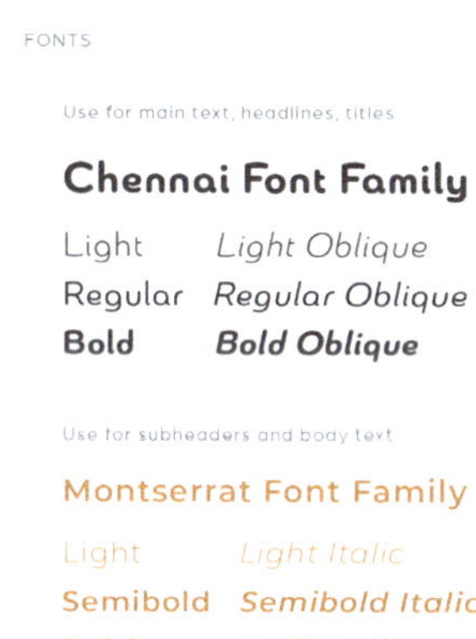

Images

If room allows on your one page style guide, you can include guidance on images or graphics that support your brand. The look and feel of any photography, patterns, icons, and so on that are used in conjunction with your brand should be a reflection of the already established style.

Compiling all of this information into one page will give anyone a quick reference guide to your brand's most essential pieces. Remember, creating consistency is key to brand recognition, and a style guide is a great step to do just that.

Feel free to use this guide as a template to create your own style guides, and remember a style guide can grow to be the length of a novel, and you will probably find yourself adding things to it as time goes on, but this one page option is a great place to start.

BONUS ONE

Logo Design Questionnaire for Clients

I have learned a lot in my two decades of logo design, and I still cannot predict what logo a client will choose! It is important to give them options and adapt your designs based on their feedback. After all, the client is always 'right,' in that it is ultimately their logo, and they have to love it.

One thing that has been incredibly helpful is to have a logo design questionnaire. This document accomplishes several important tasks. First, it is a quick and easy way to start one of the toughest design projects. Working with a blank canvas for a logo design is no easy feat, and having something to use to start from will prove quite helpful. It is also nice to refer back to as you go to ensure you are staying true to the client's initial vision.

Another thing that this questionnaire has allowed me to accomplish is to have the client examine what they are trying to accomplish. Oftentimes a client has not really thought through a lot of the things these questions bring up. From who their ideal audience is to what colors they are not fond of, and so on, these questions get their mind focused on what is ultimately vital to a successful logo design.

This questionnaire is yours to use as you see fit for your logo design projects. Typically, I email them a fillable PDF copy, but I have also used an online form, so feel free to adapt it to what works for you.

LOGO DESIGN QUESTIONNAIRE

Please fill these out as **thoroughly** as you can.

YOUR BUSINESS

What is the name of your business?

Describe your business or service in **one sentence.**

Who are your main competitors and how do you differ from them?

What do you like or dislike about your competitor's branding?

YOUR LOGO

Do you have a specific idea in mind for your logo?

Do you want to use specific colors or a particular range of colors?

LOGO DESIGN QUESTIONNAIRE

Please fill these out as **thoroughly** as you can.

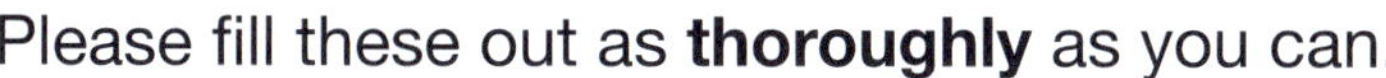

YOUR BUSINESS

What is the name of your business?

Describe your business or service in **one sentence.**

Who are your main competitors and how do you differ from them?

What do you like or dislike about your competitor's branding?

YOUR LOGO

Do you have a specific idea in mind for your logo?

Do you want to use specific colors or a particular range of colors?

Are there any colors that you do **NOT** want to use?

Do you have a particular **font** you would like to use?

Do you have a particular font you would **NOT** like to use?

What words should describe your logo?

What message or emotion do you want your logo to portray?

Does your logo have a **tag line**? If yes, what is it?

Is your tag line to appear with your logo on all of your branding?

Where will your logo predominantly be used?

What logos do you like and why?

Is your logo going to be used more in print or web or both?

Any other comments?

BONUS TWO

Mock Client Logo Projects

Use these logo design briefs to practice and hone your skills, not to mention add content to your portfolio!

LOGO DESIGN BRIEF #1

Company Name: Pennants
Company Details: We are a flag design company that specializes in custom flag creation, as well as geographical flag distribution.
Tagline: Fly the Flags
Color Style Preference: Blue and purple
Logo Style Preference: Combination
Logo Usage: Online. Print.

LOGO DESIGN BRIEF #2

Company Name: Swiftcharge
Company Details: We are a small company that develops new ways to make payments using our main product, which is an app. Our target audience is young females, and we want to convey a sense of empowerment, as well as a down-to-earth feel.
Tagline: Swipe with confidence
Color Style Preference: Teal
Logo Style Preference: Wordmark
Logo Usage: Digital mostly.

LOGO DESIGN BRIEF #3

Company Name: Elitique
Company Details: We are a luxury store that sells beauty products. Our target audience is females who want to spend a little more for quality. We want to convey a feeling of sophistication.
Tagline: Be Inspired.
Color Style Preference: Hues of pink
Logo Style Preference: Combination
Logo Usage: Signage. Online. Print.

LOGO DESIGN BRIEF #4

Company Name: Quick Fix Computers
Company Details: We are an online service that provides house calls to repair computer issues. Our main clientele are homeowners, both male and female. We want our brand to be fun and easy to recognize.
Tagline: We make everything better
Color Style Preference: Lime green and gray
Logo Style Preference: Any
Logo Usage: Online. Print.

Mock Client Logo Projects

LOGO DESIGN BRIEF #5

Company Name: BubblePen
Company Details: We are a company that makes and distributes comic books. They are available in stores worldwide. Our target audience is students. We want to convey a sense of bravery, while at the same time being lively.
Tagline: We're serious about comic books
Color Style Preference: Green
Logo Style Preference: Combination
Logo Usage: Signage. Online. Print.

LOGO DESIGN BRIEF #6

Company Name: SoolaBites
Company Details: We are a company that makes and distributes vegan desserts. Our target audience is vegan females and males. We want to convey health and organic elements.
Tagline: Have a break. Have dessert.
Color Style Preference: Reds
Logo Style Preference: Abstract
Logo Usage: Online. Print.

LOGO DESIGN BRIEF #7

Company Name: Material Maven
Company Details: We are a big chain of stores that sells fabrics. Our main product stands out because of its superior quality. Our target audience is seniors. We want to convey a sense of comfort, while at the same time being fresh and innovative.
Tagline: Quality Always Wins
Color Style Preference: Oranges and yellows.
Logo Style Preference: Abstract or Lettermark.
Logo Usage: Online. Print.

LOGO DESIGN BRIEF #8

Company Name: Elegant Escapes
Company Details: We are a travel company, and we offer a variety of high end destinations. We are able to offer exclusive hotel deals because of our staff of travel experts. Our target audience is adults. We want to convey a sense of comfort, while at the same time being high end and professional.
Tagline: Travel at its Finest
Color Style Preference: Shades of blue
Logo Style Preference: Emblem
Logo Usage: Signage. Online. Print.

Mock Client Logo Projects

LOGO DESIGN BRIEF #9

Company Name: ECONOLOFT
Company Details: We are a company that offers a selection of afforable apartments with great prices. Our target audience is young married couples. We want to convey quality and affordability.
Tagline: Affordable Living in Style
Color Style Preference: Greens/Blues
Logo Style Preference: Any
Logo Usage: Signage. Online. Print.

LOGO DESIGN BRIEF #10

Company Name: Tossmasters
Company Details: We are a company that creates ultimate frisbee lessons for beginners. Our target audience is parents. We want to convey fun and value.
Tagline: Learn to Throw Like a Pro
Color Style Preference: Red, Orange
Logo Style Preference: Would like to see options.
Logo Usage: Online. Print.

LOGO DESIGN BRIEF #11

Company Name: High Roads Pro
Company Details: We are a company that makes premium all-terrain vehicles, with an emphasis on form over function. Our target audience is men. We want to convey a sense of adventure.
Tagline: Premium All-Terrain Vehicles
Color Style Preference: Blues/Grays
Logo Style Preference: Combination
Logo Usage: Online. Print.

LOGO DESIGN BRIEF #12

Company Name: Fresh Choice
Company Details: We are a little corner-shop that sells groceries. The main difference between us and our competitors is our customer service and quality standards. Our target audience is local people who live alone. We want to convey affordable, small portion groceries.
Tagline: Quality Groceries For All
Color Style Preference: Any
Logo Style Preference: Any
Logo Usage: Signage. Online. Print.

Mock Client Logo Projects

LOGO DESIGN BRIEF #13

Company Name: Firelight Furnishings
Company Details: We are a family store that sells lighting fixtures. Our main product stands out because of its reputation and homemade feel. Our target audience is homeowners. We want to convey a sense of rustic modernness.
Tagline: Be inspired.
Color Style Preference: Browns/Tans
Logo Style Preference: Combination or abstract.
Logo Usage: Signage. Online. Print.

LOGO DESIGN BRIEF #14

Company Name: Coding Clips
Company Details: We make educational YouTube series for learning computer science. We pride ourselves on our thorough yet quick videos. Our target audience is teens and young adults. We want to convey a sense of fun while learning.
Tagline: Computer Classes for Kids
Color Style Preference: Any but pink
Logo Style Preference: Abstract or Wordmark, maybe Lettermark options
Logo Usage: Online mostly. Print.

LOGO DESIGN BRIEF #15

Company Name: Greener Steps
Company Details: We are a fashion company that sells sustainable footwear. Our items are quality made, but with a quick turnaround. Our target audience is famlies. We want to convey a sense of quality, but with visual appeal.
Tagline: Step forward together.
Color Style Preference: Open to any
Logo Style Preference: Maybe mascot
Logo Usage: Online. Print.

LOGO DESIGN BRIEF #16

Company Name: Boardly
Company Details: We are a family store that sells board games. Our games are not found in larger stores, but are more specific. Our target audience is friends/families. We want to convey a sense of fun and surprise.
Tagline: Not your average board games.
Color Style Preference: Oranges/Blues
Logo Style Preference: Combination, Wordmark, or Abstract
Logo Usage: Signage. Online. Print.

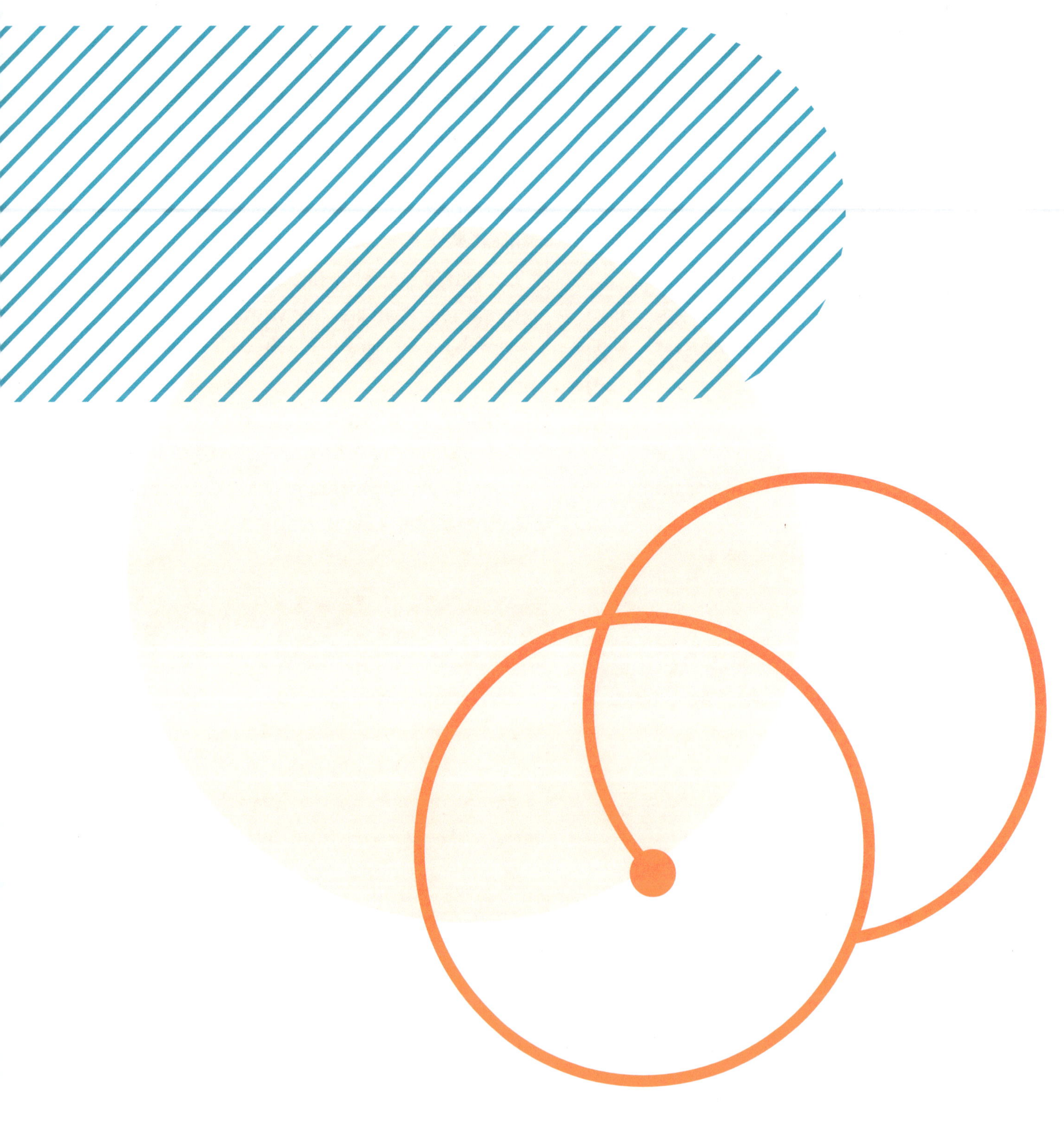

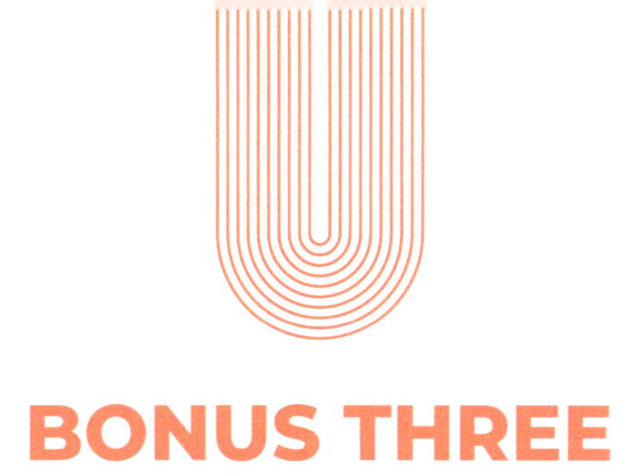

BONUS THREE

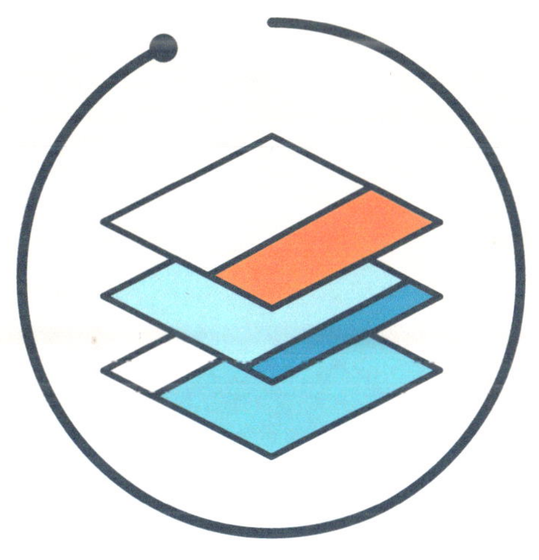

ADOBE *Illustrator*

GUIDE

MEET ADOBE *Illustrator*

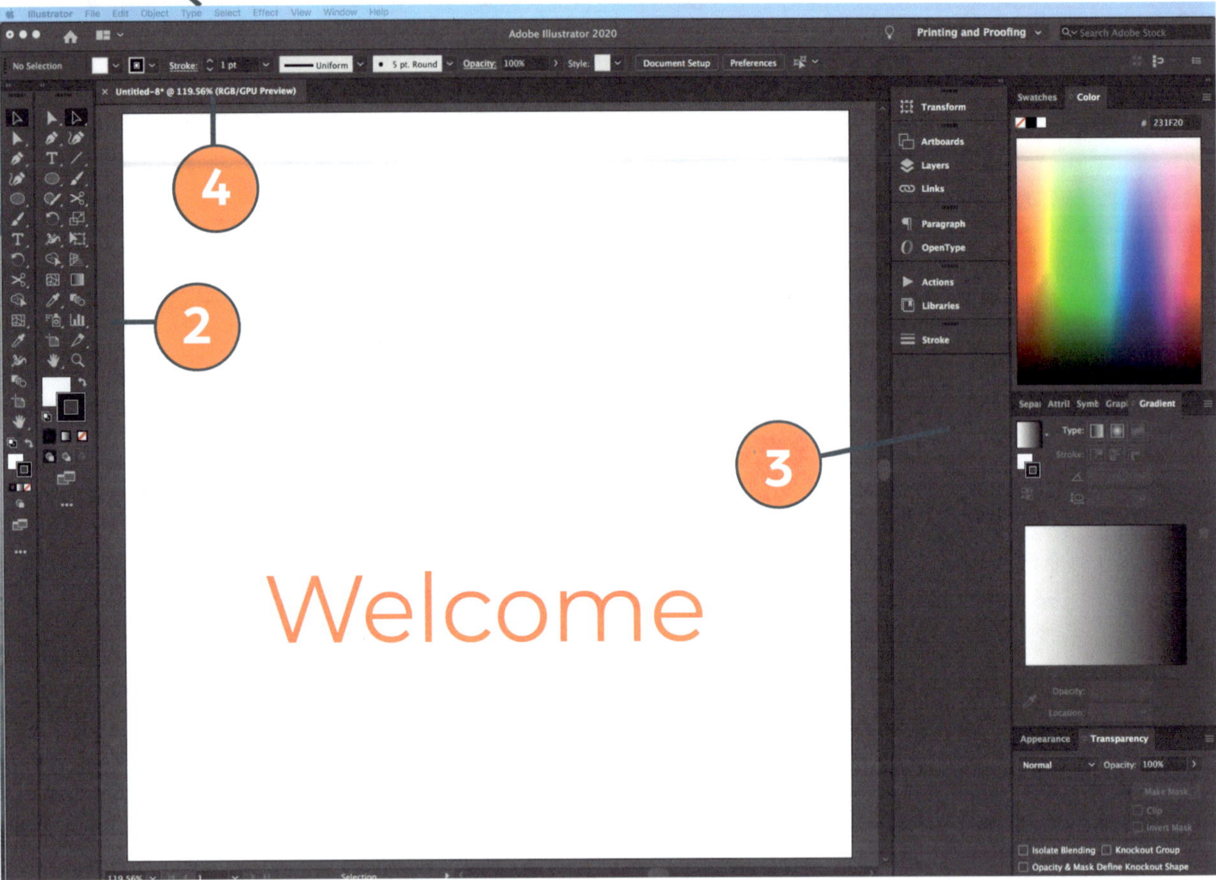

1. **The Menu Bar:** Includes the File, Edit, and other menus that give you access to a variety of commands, adjustments, settings, and panels.

2. **Tools Panel:** Contains the tools for creating and editing artwork. You can customize the tools that display here and there are additional tools that display in the ones with the white corner triangle that you can access by holding down the mouse over that tool.

3. **Panels:** These contain different controls to edit your artwork including Properties, Layers, and Artboards. You can customize displays with what is most helpful to your current project.

4. **Document Window:** Displays the file you're currently working on.

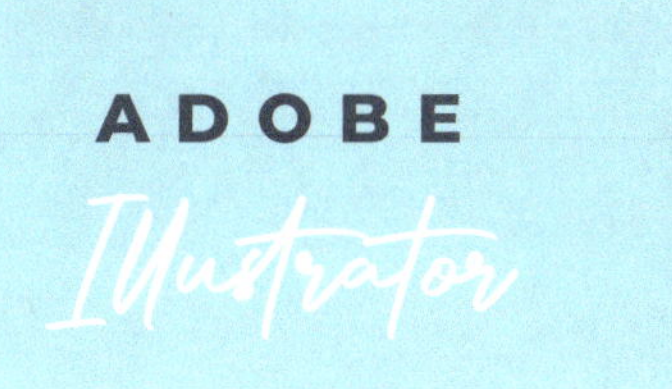

Tool Panel & Shortcuts

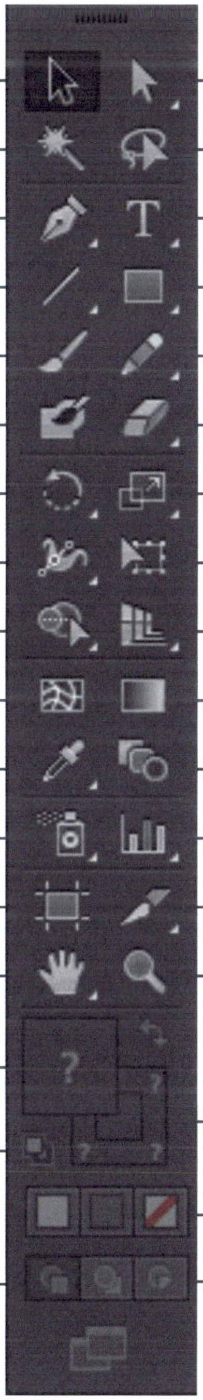

Selection Tool (V)	Direct Selection Tool (A)
Magic Wand Tool (Y)	Lasso Tool (Q)
Pen Tool (P)	Type Tool (T)
Line Segment Tool (\)	Rectangle Tool (M)
Paintbrush Tool (B)	Pencil Tool (N)
Blob Brush Tool (Shift + B)	Eraser Tool (Shift + E)
Rotate Tool (R)	Scale Tool (S)
Width Tool (Shift + W)	Free Transform Tool (E)
Shape Builder Tool (Shift + M)	Perspective Grid Tool (Shift + P)
Mesh Tool (U)	Gradient Tool (G)
Eyedropper Tool (I)	Blend Tool (W)
Symbol Sprayer Tool (Shift + S)	Column Graph Tool (J)
Artboard Tool (Shift + O)	Slice Tool (Shift + K)
Hand Tool (H)	Zoom Tool (Z)
Fill Color	
Default Fill and Stroke (D)	Stroke Color
	Fill Options
Drawing Modes	Change Screen Mode (F)

ADOBE
Illustrator

Common Shortcuts

Function	MAC	Windows
Create a new document	Command + N	Ctrl + N
Open a document	Command + O	Ctrl + O
Save a document	Command + S	Ctrl + S
View at 100%	Command + 1	Ctrl +1
Fit to screen	Command + 0	Ctrl + 0
Zoom in	Command + (+)	Ctrl + (+)
Zoom out	Command + (–)	Ctrl + (–)
Duplicate an object	Option + drag	Alt + drag
Revert a doc to original	F12	F12
Toggle screen modes	F	F
Default fill/stroke colors	D	D
Toggle fill/stroke	X	X
Lock selection	Command + 2	Ctrl + 2
Lock all artwork	Command + Shift + Option + 2	Ctrl + Shift + Alt + 2
Unlock all artwork	Command + Option + 2	Ctrl + Alt + 2
Align paragraph(s) center	Command + Shift + C	Ctrl + Shift + C
Align paragraph(s) left	Command + Shift + L	Ctrl + Shift + L
Align paragraph(s) right	Command + Shift + R	Ctrl + Shift + R
Justify paragraph(s)	Command + Shift + J	Ctrl + Shift + J
Insert soft return	Shift + Enter	Shift + Enter

ADOBE

Illustrator

Useful File Formats

AI

Adobe Illustrator's standard vector file format.
Useful to always keep a source file in this format for any project.

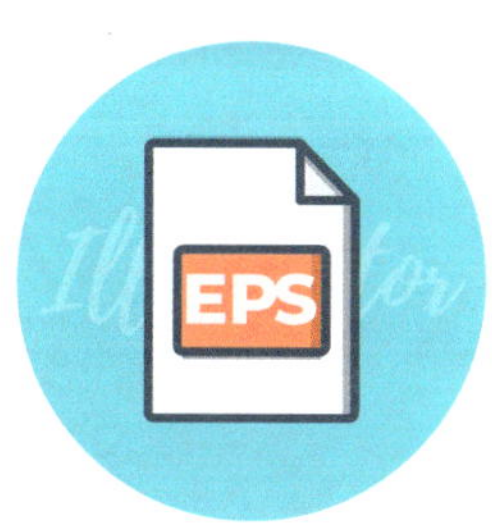

EPS

EPS is a PostScript image file format.
Since it is compatible with other graphics applications, it can be used to transfer files to individuals who may not be using Illustrator.

SVG

Scalable Vector Graphics (SVG)
An XML-based vector image format for 2D graphics. It is also compatible with graphics applications other than Illustrator, so it is often used for file transfers.

PDF

Adobe's Portable Document Format.
Unlike other PDFs, this particular format preserves all the data in the original file. Ideal whenever you're trying to open artwork in different Creative Cloud apps.

Useful Features

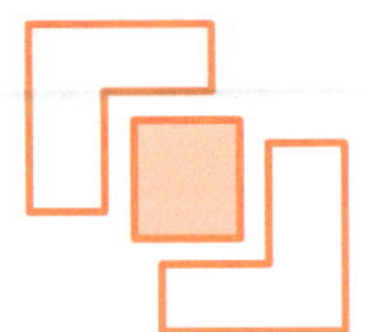

Pathfinder

These tools allow you to combine objects into new shapes with options like Unite, Divide, and Trim.

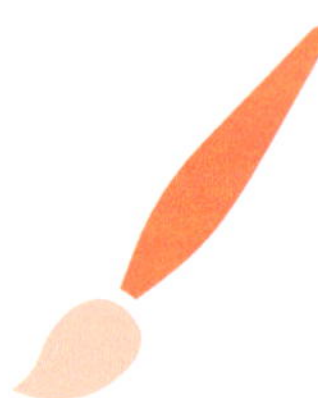

Brushes

You can change the appearance of a path with a brush. There are different types of brushes to achieve different effects: calligraphic, scatter, art, pattern, and bristle.

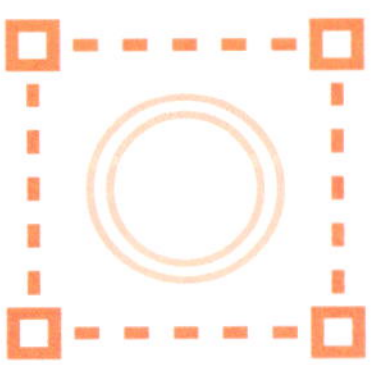

Convert Text to Outlines

You can convert any text (typed using a font) into vector artwork. Create outlines of any text, but once you do this you cannot edit the text, and can only edit the now vector shaped letters.
Shortcut: select the text and shift + command + O

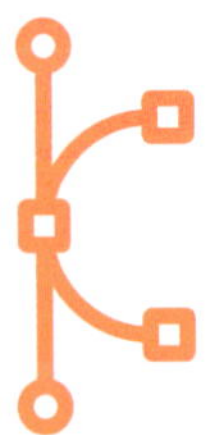

Image Trace

Use this tool to turn an existing piece of artwork (like a raster image or a drawing you made) into a vector object. Choose from different modes like B&W, line art, or color, and tweak the different options to create varying levels of detail.

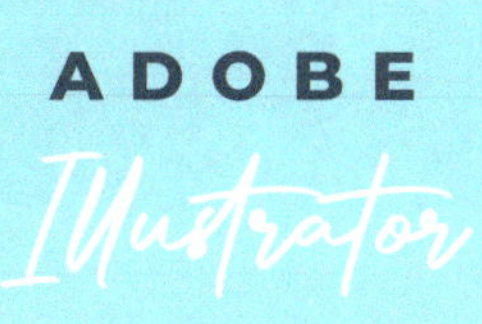

The Pen Tools

How to Use the Pen Tool to Create Lines

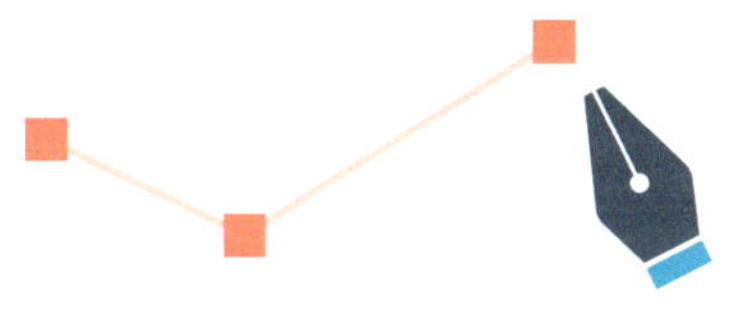

Pen Tool – Straight Lines

Select the Pen Tool, click to create points, and they'll connect to form straight lines. You can add a point to close these lines, forming a closed shape.

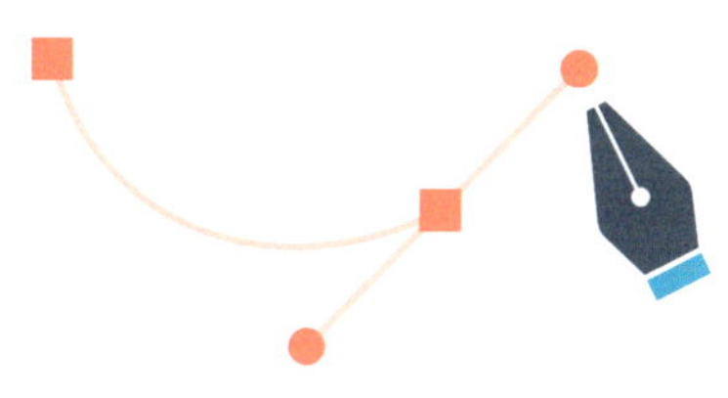

Create Curved Lines

While you are creating individual points with the Pen Tool, you can click and drag any one of those points to add what is called Bezier handles. These can be dragged to change the curve.

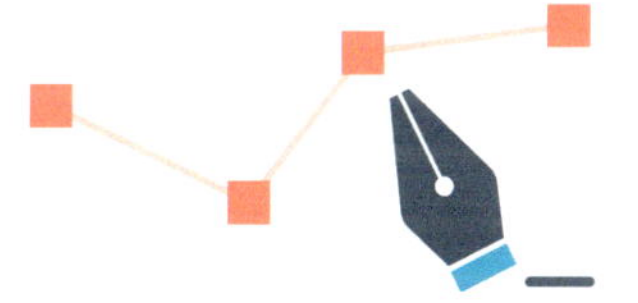

Delete Anchor Point Tool

Hover over any point you've created and simply click to delete it.

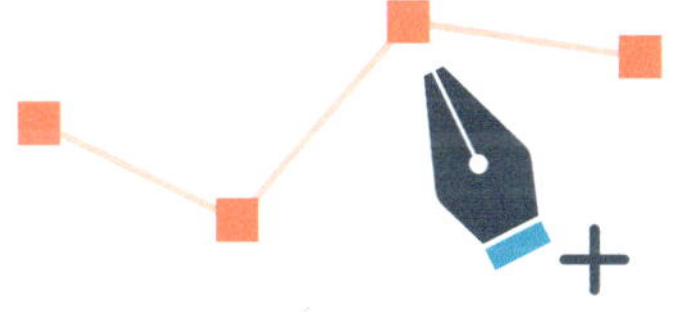

Add Anchor Point Tool

Hover over a section of a line, and the cursor will display the option to add a new point.

Anchor Point Tool

Hover over any anchor point for the option to select and alter it.

The Selection Tools

Different Options for Manipulating an Object

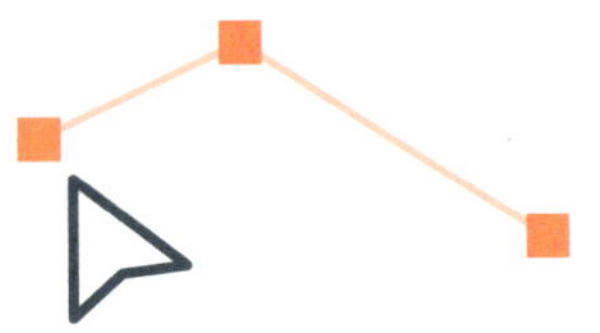

Selection Tool (V)

Click on any object, line, or shape to select it.

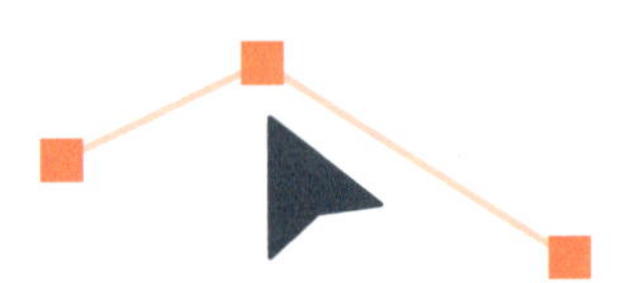

Direct Selection Tool (A)

Use this to move individual points in your shapes or line segments.

Shortcut: hold down COMMAND/CTRL while using the default Selection tool.

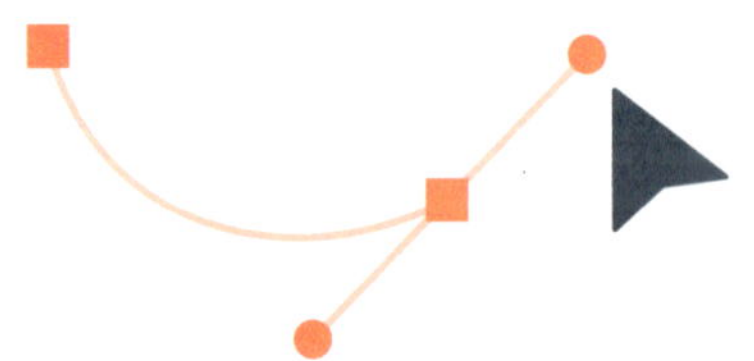

Move Bezier Handles

With the same Direct Selection tool, you can adjust Bezier handles to change curves.

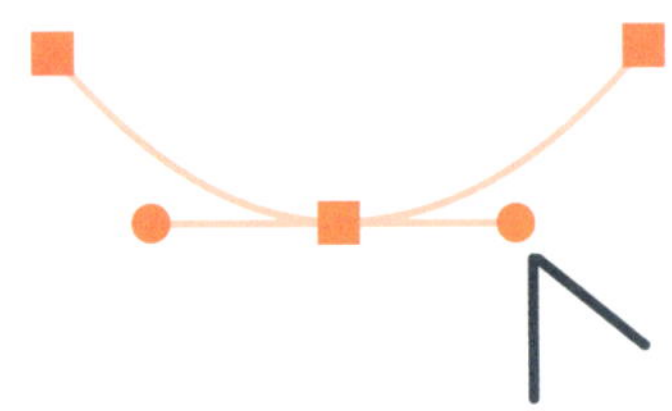

Turn a Straight Line into a Curved Line

Use the Anchor Point tool to click and hold the point you want to change until handles appear, creating a curved (Bezier) line.

Shortcut: hold OPTION/ALT while using the Pen Tool.

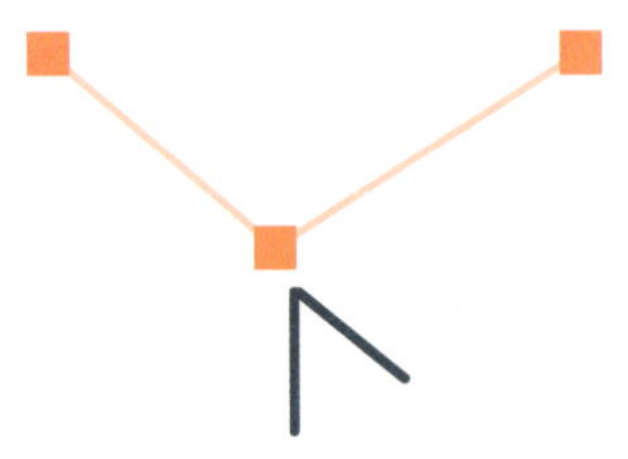

Turning Curves into Straight Lines

You can use the same Anchor Point tool to remove handles and turn your curve into a straight line.

The Type Tools

Use these tools to add text to your document.

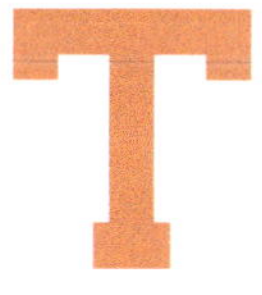

Type Tool (T)
Use this tool to click and add text to any document. Drag the tool to create a text container.

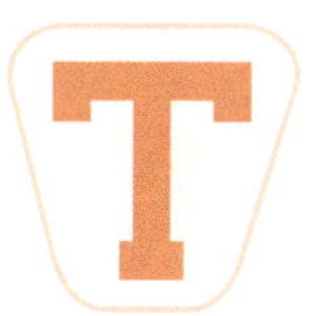

Area Type Tool
This allows you to convert an existing shape into a text box and type in it.

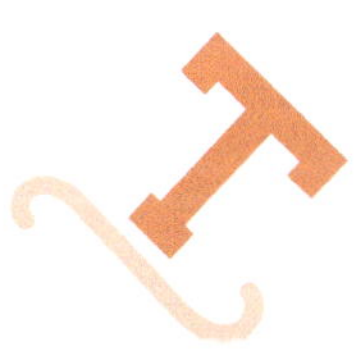

Type on a Path Tool
This tool allows you to use an existing line or shape as a path to type on. Simply click on the path to add editable text.

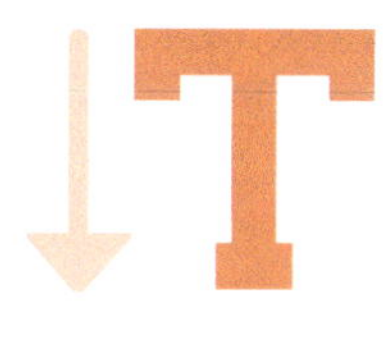

Vertical Type Tool
This tool allows you to type your text vertically instead of horizontally.

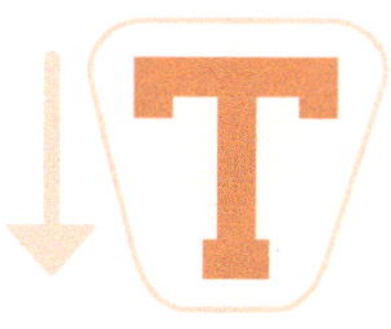

Vertical Area Type Tool
Just like the area type tool, but it allows you to type vertically instead of horizontally.

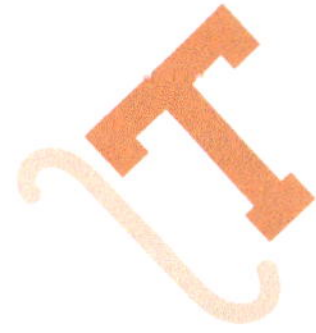

Vertical Type on a Path Tool
Just like the type on a path tool, but it allows you to type vertically instead of horizontally.

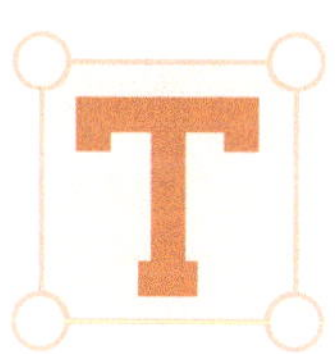

Touch Type Tool
This allows you to select individual letters of existing text and move them around.

Other Tools

Curvature Tool (shift+)
The curvature tool is an awesome way to create vector shapes, especially those with curved edges.

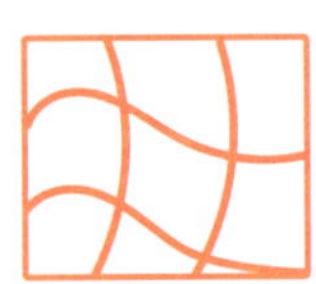

Mesh Tool (U)
This tool allows you to select certain points within a specific section of your shape to add another color, allowing the colors to combine into a gradient effect, acting as highlights, shading, and natural color progression.

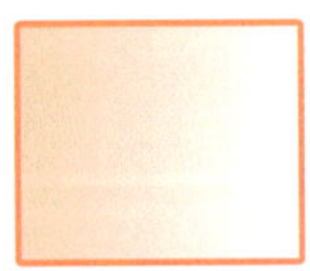

Gradient Tool (G)
This tool creates either linear or radial gradients within a shape or line.

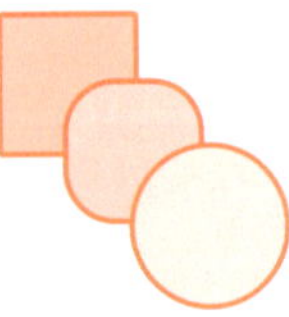

Blend Tool (W)
This tool allows you to take two different colored objects and create a gradient blend between them.

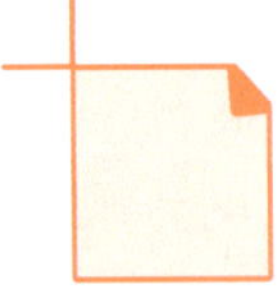

Artboard Tool (shift+O)
Use this tool to add a new artboard or resize your current artboards.

Zoom Tool (Z)
The zoom tool zooms in and out of your workspace.

JUMP IN!

Start Designing!

Creating a New Illustrator Document

Open Adobe Illustrator.

1 When you open Illustrator, you'll see the Start workspace. Click **Create new** to open the New Document dialog box, or simply press Control+N (Windows) or Command+N, (macOS) or you can simply click on one of the **presets** provided at the top.

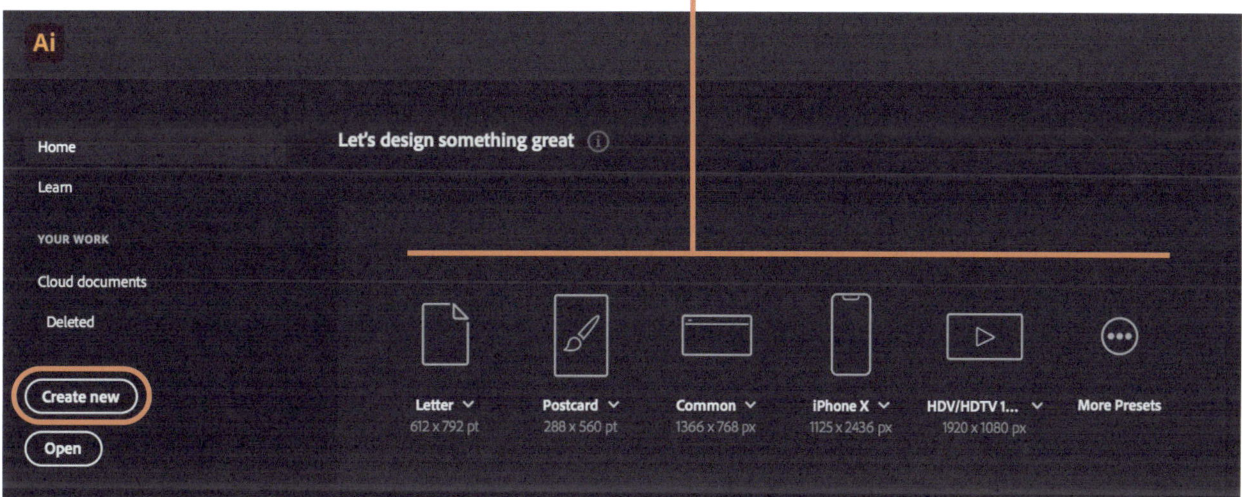

2 Select a category at the top such as Print, Mobile, or Web. These presets will prove very helpful in suggesting color modes, sizes, resolution, etc.

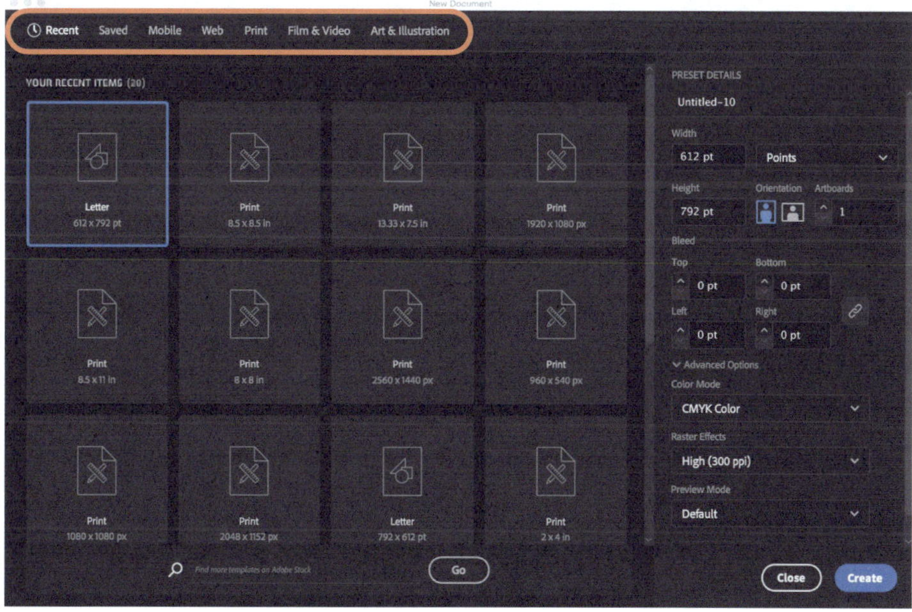

Tip: Decide on your project before choosing a category. Choose Print if you're designing a flyer, business card, or logo; choose Web if you plan to work on a web banner, social graphic, or art for your blog. If you're unsure of the final destination, select Art & Illustration and customize the settings for your project.

3 Once you select a category, you'll see presets for commonly used document types. This can be a great starting point to create a blank document using predefined dimensions and settings. For example, after picking Print, you can select a letter size file.

4 You can customize your document on the right side, whether or not you picked a preset. In the panel on the right, you can specify exact dimensions, alter measurement units, page orientation, add a print bleed, etc.

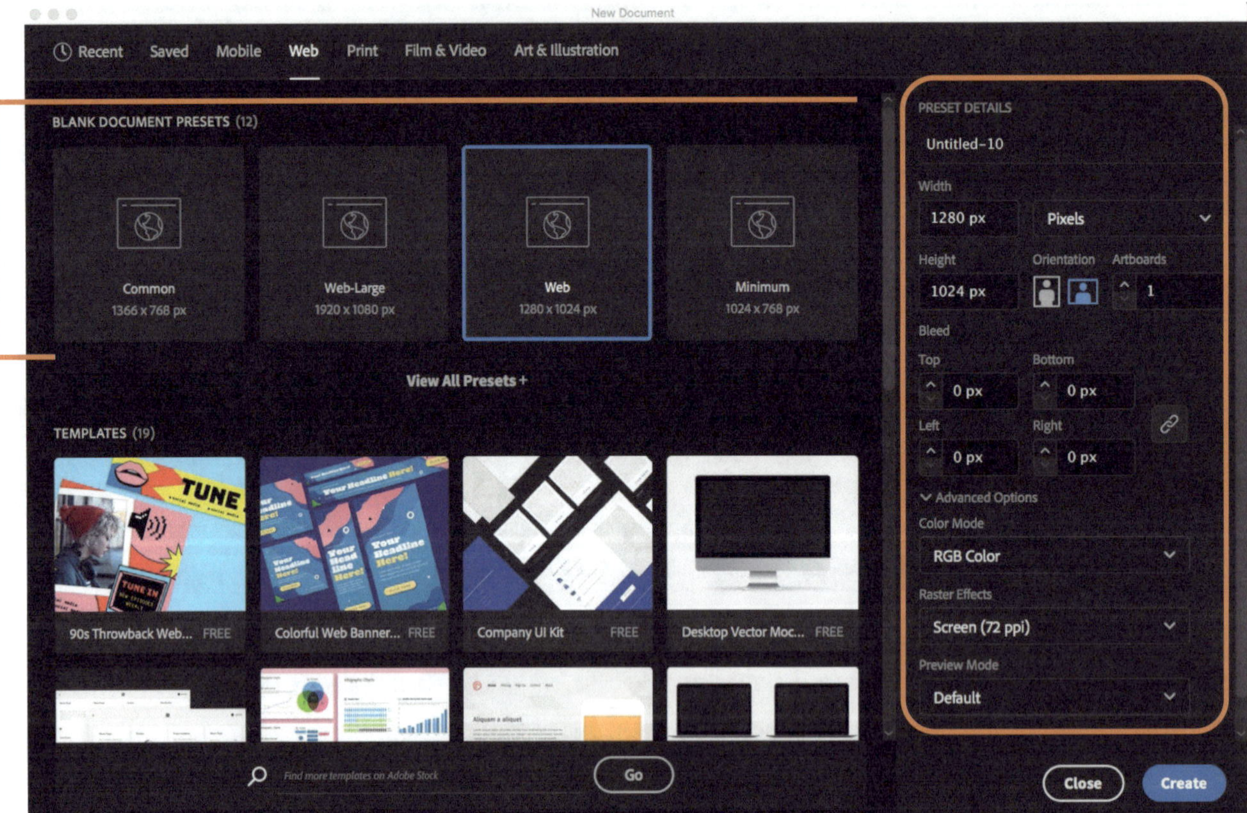

5 When you're ready, click **Create**. This will open a new document with a blank artboard all set up and ready for you.

You can change the settings at any point. Details on how to change them can be found on the next pages.

Edit an artboard

An artboard is like your canvas for your creations. Artboards can be of any size and your document can actually contain numerous artboards which can also be different sizes, so you can easily design for different projects and output sizes all at once.

If your **Properties** panel is not visible, go to the Window menu and select **Properties**. With nothing selected in your document, click **Edit Artboards** (as shown).

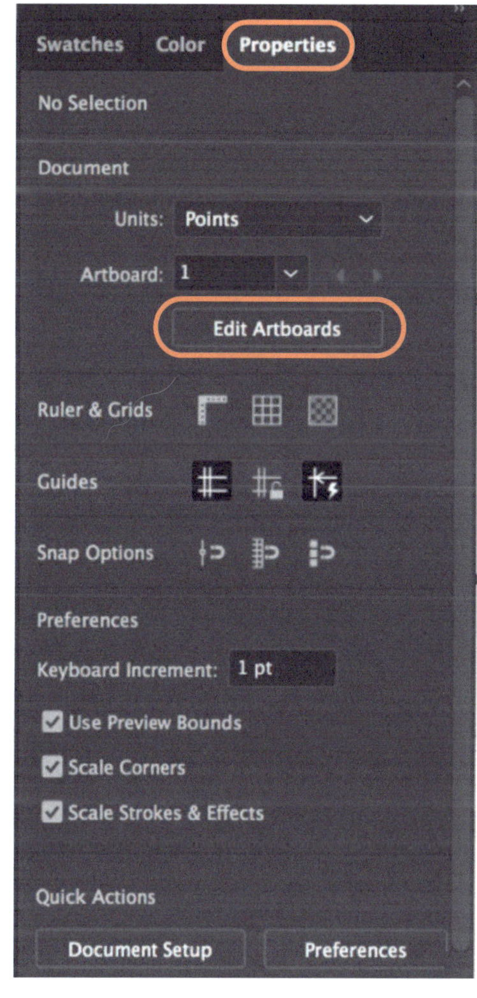

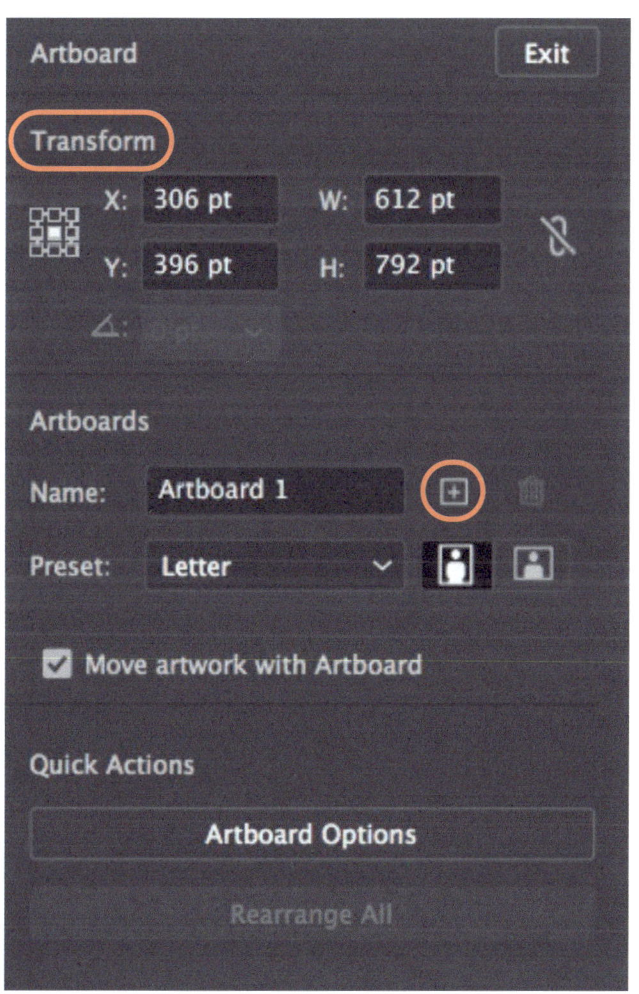

You can edit the width and height of the artboard by typing new values in the boxes under Transform. Click the New Artboard icon (highlighted) to create additional artboards. You can select a preset from the drop down. Click an artboard to select it and you can manually adjust it by dragging the edges, or delete it by pressing the delete key.

When you're done making edits, press Esc or click the Exit button at the top of the Properties panel.

Edit the document

It is easy to make a change to your entire document consisting of numerous artboards. In the **Properties** panel, click **Document Setup** under **Quick Actions**. Change the units or bleed settings, and then click OK.

Another option is to click **Preferences** in the **Properties** panel to access and edit any of the Illustrator application settings to your preference. (These preferences are saved when you quit Illustrator.)

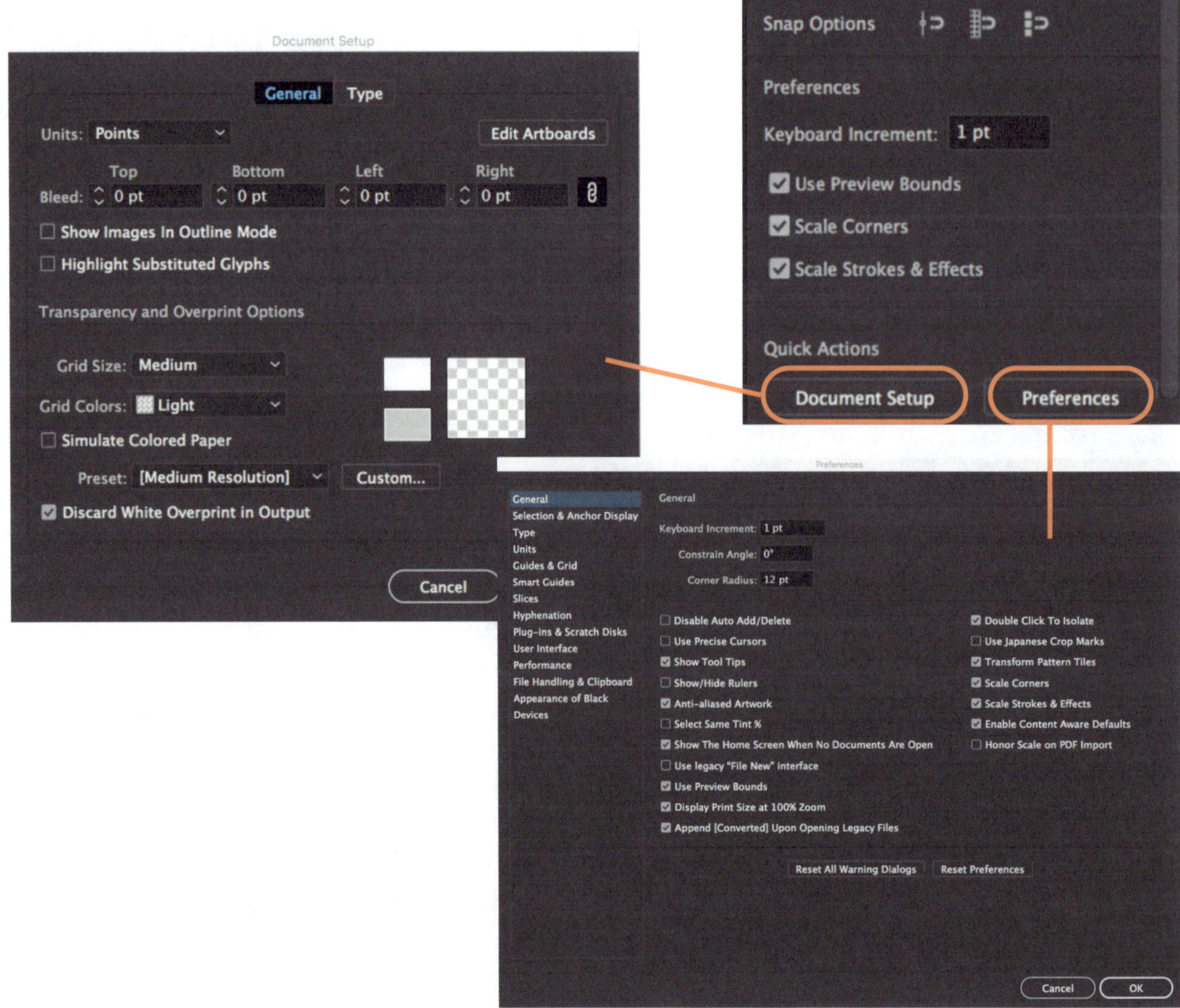

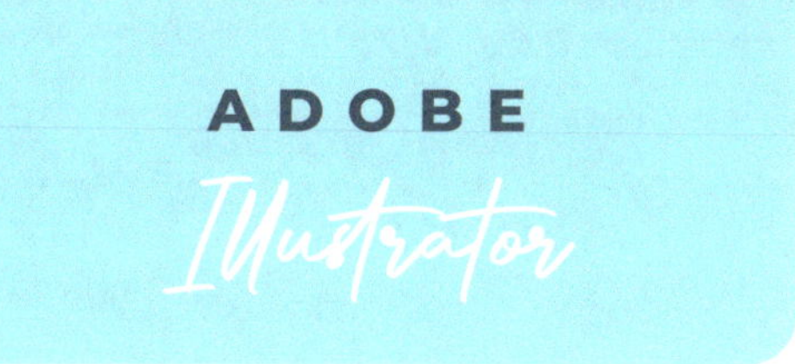

Expanded Tools

Note the shortcut keyboard letters next to each tool – these are essential to learn for the most common tools.

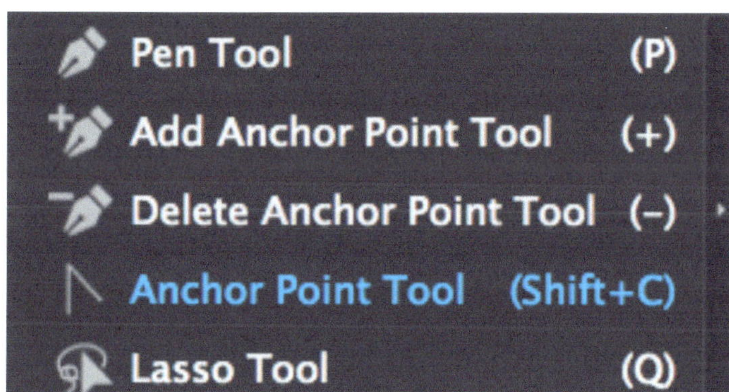

These tools are explained further on the Pen Tools page.

Lasso Tool (Q)

This works like the Direct Selection Tool, allowing you to select individual anchor points within a shape or object, but it works by drawing a shape around the points you want selected, making it a breeze to select multiple points at one time.

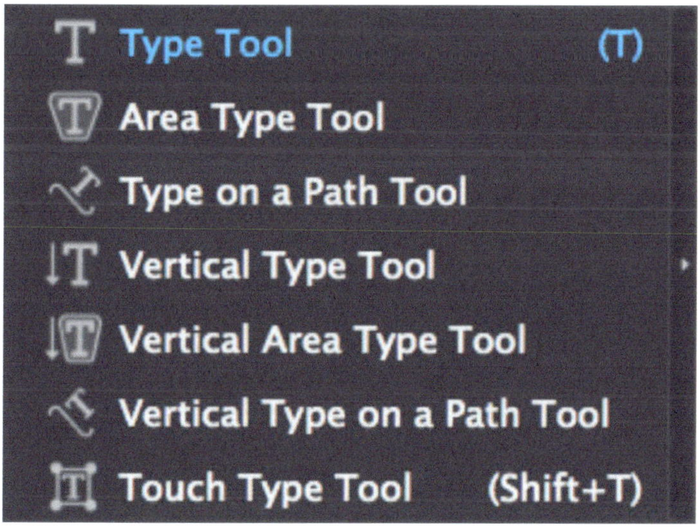

These tools are for adding text to your document.

These tools are explained in further detail on the Text Tools page.

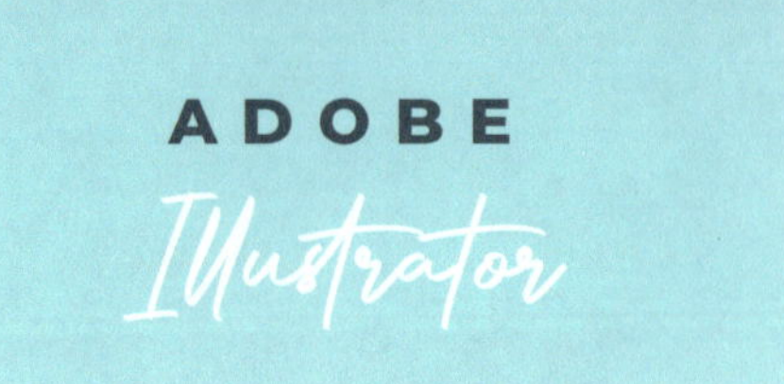

Expanded Tools

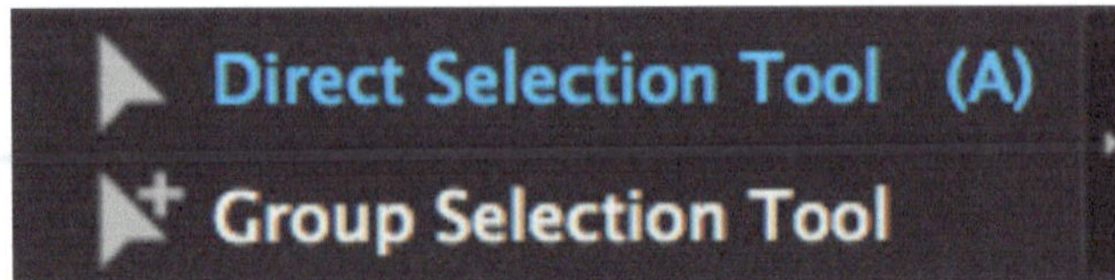

Direct Selection Tool (A)

The direct selection tool allows you to individually select and edit specific anchor points of vector shapes or lines.

Group Selection Tool

This tool allows you to easily select a specific object within a group in order to move, edit, or resize it individually.

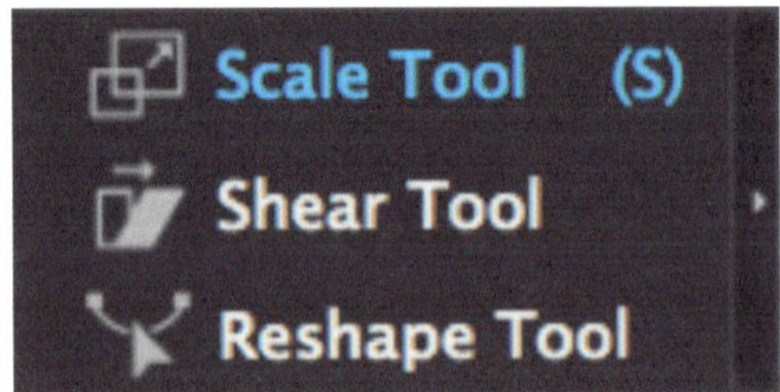

Scale Tool (S)

This tool scales objects up using the center point as a marker. Hold down shift to constrain your proportions.

Shear Tool

This tool skews your objects at an angle. Hold down shift to constrain proportions.

Reshape Tool

This tool allows you to select multiple anchor points on a line or shape and move them all in one direction.

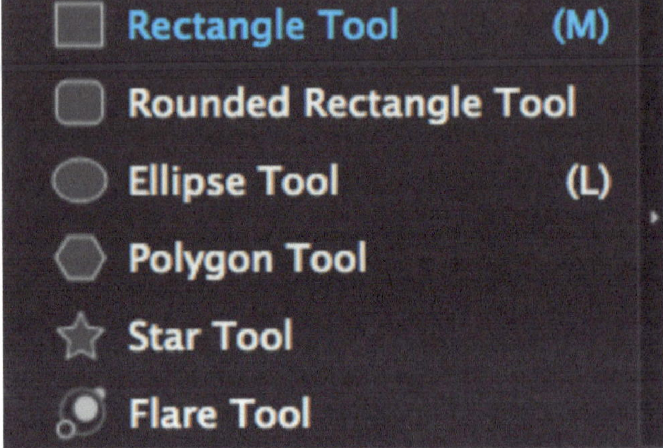

Rectangle Tool (M)

Used to create squares and rectangles.

Rounded Rectangle Tool

The same as the rectangle tool but with rounded corners.

Ellipse Tool (L)

Circles and ovals are created with this.

Polygon Tool

Use this to create any polygon from triangles to octagons and so on.

Star Tool

This makes stars! You can adjust the number of points on the star and how far the inner points go in.

Flare Tool

Not often used, this tool does just what it says: it creates a flare shape.

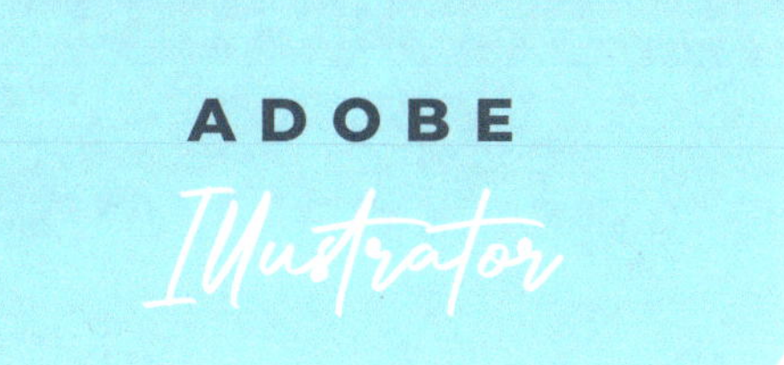

Expanded Tools

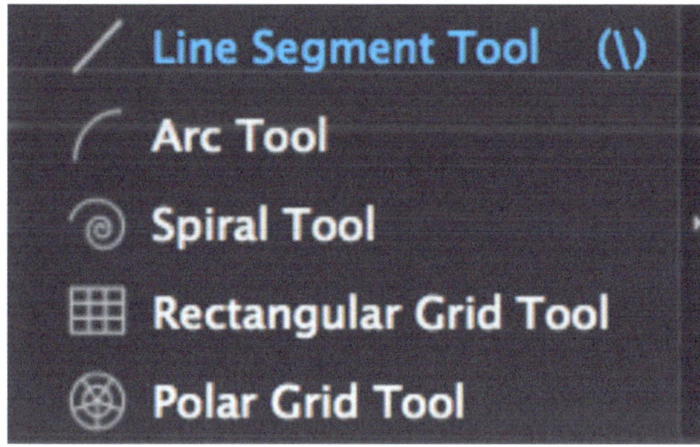

Line Segment Tool (\)
This tool creates individual lines. Hold down shift to keep them at 45 degree angles.

Arc Tool
Another way to create a arc or segment of an oval/circle.

Spiral Tool
Creates a spiral if you ever find yourself needing a spiral!

Rectangular Grid Tool
This tool is super handy to create a table that you can then edit the elements using the anchor points as well as change colors, line weights, etc.

Polar Grid Tool
This tool creates a round grid – kind of like a burner on a stove – if you find yourself needing such a thing.

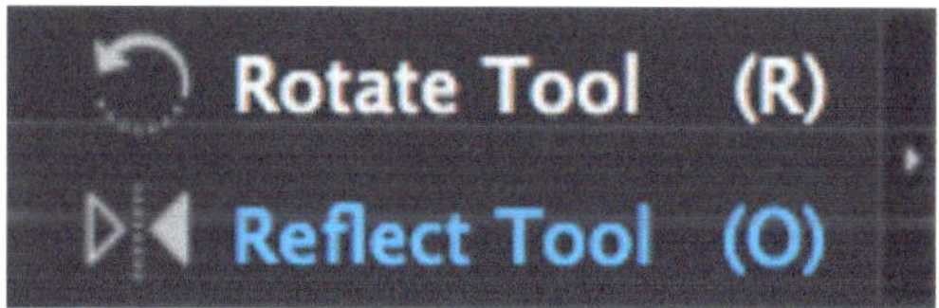

Rotate Tool (R)
This tool allows you to rotate shapes.

Reflect Tool (O)
This tool rotates an object as well but in a reflected state. Hold down shift to reflect it horizontally.

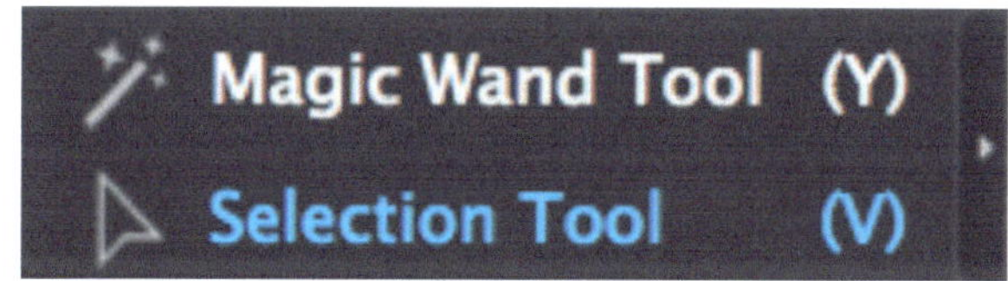

Magic Wand Tool (Y)
Use this tool to click on a single object, and then automatically select everything else in your workspace with that same color.

Selection Tool (V)
This is the main selection tool, and you will find yourself using the shortcut (V) very often!

Expanded Tools

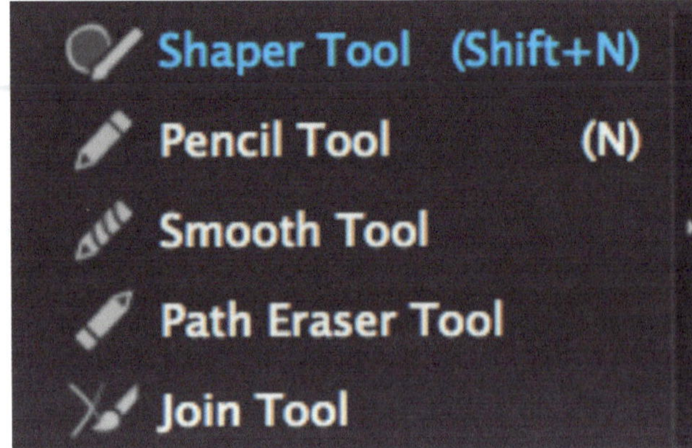

Shaper Tool (Shift+N)

This handy tool transforms your general shape into a cleaned up solid version. Try it!

Pencil Tool (N)

This acts similarly to the Paintbrush tool allowing freehand drawing.

Smooth Tool

This tool does just what it says and smooths out lines.

Path Eraser Tool

This allows you to erase part of a line.

Join Tool

This allows you to take two individual paths and merge them into one single path. Just select both paths and then use this tool to join them.

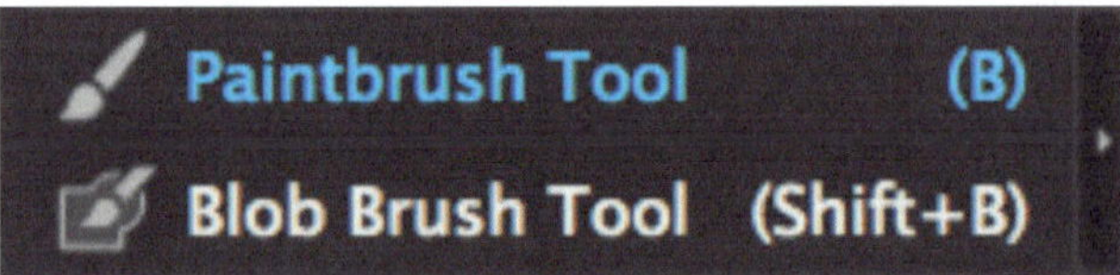

Paintbrush Tool (B)

Another letter you will find yourself typing a lot is the shortcut (B) to access this handy paintbrush tool.

Blob Brush Tool (Shift+B)

This is like the paintbrush tool but it creates a vector shape around the brushstroke creating an area instead of a path.

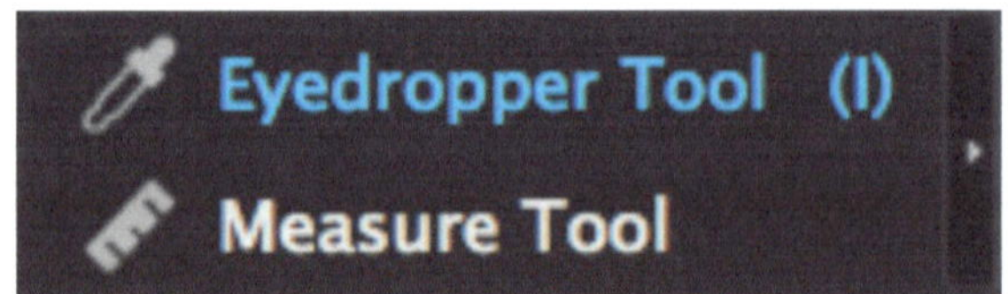

Eyedropper Tool (I)

This tool allows you to sample colors from shapes, lines, objects, or images so you can use that same color in other parts of your design.

Measure Tool

This tool allows you to click and drag between two points to measure the distance.

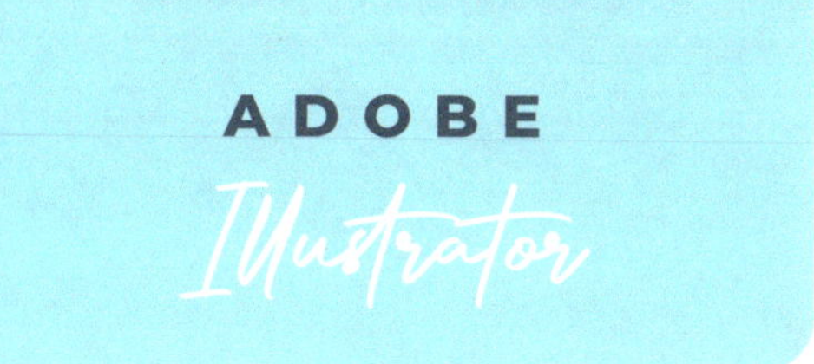

Expanded Tools

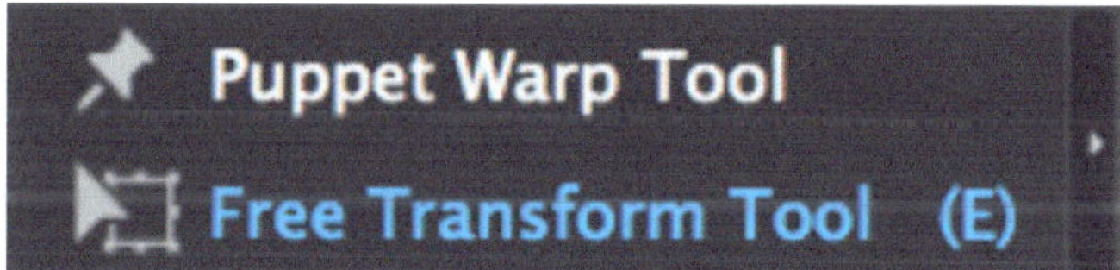

Puppet Warp Tool

The Puppet Warp tool lets you twist and distort parts of your artwork. With it, you can add, move, and rotate pins to seamlessly transform your artwork into different variations.

Free Transform Tool (E)

This allows you to resize a shape in multiple ways.

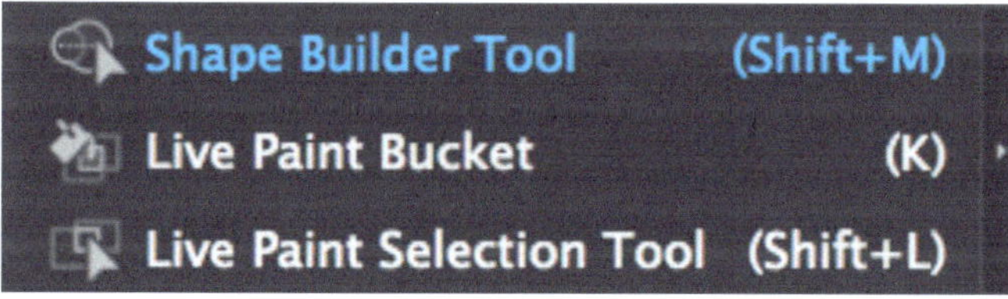

Shape Builder Tool (Shift+M)

This allows you to combine multiplc, overlapping shapes into one.

Live Paint Bucket (K)

This allows you to easily fill shapes with colors or patterns.

Live Paint Selection Tool (Shift+L)

This allows you to select individual segments for your live paint area and adjust them.

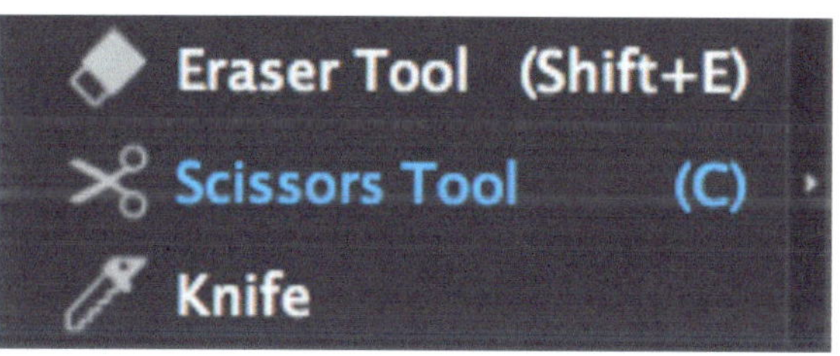

Eraser Tool (Shift+E)

Wait for it – this erases! It can be very useful in editing out a portion of an object or path.

Scissors Tool (C)

Use this tool to cut a vector path or object.

Knife

This works like the scissors tool but has more freedom in how it cuts.

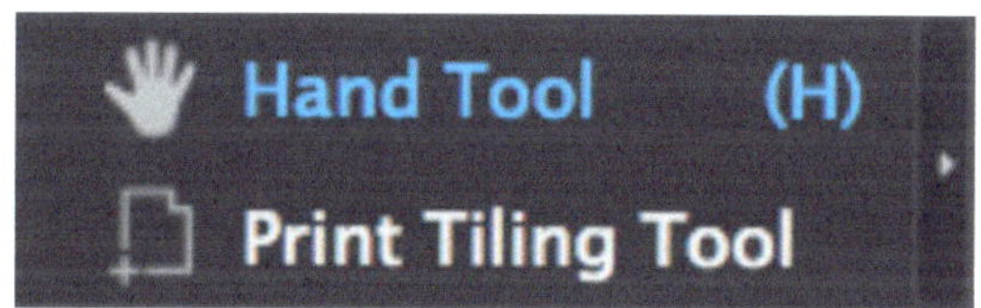

Hand Tool (H)

This is one of my favorite tools, and I type the letter H constantly. This allows you to move the view you have of your workspace.

Print Tiling Tool

This tool allows you to set up a printed item larger than a typical print area and accurately adjust how it will print on several pages.

Expanded Tools

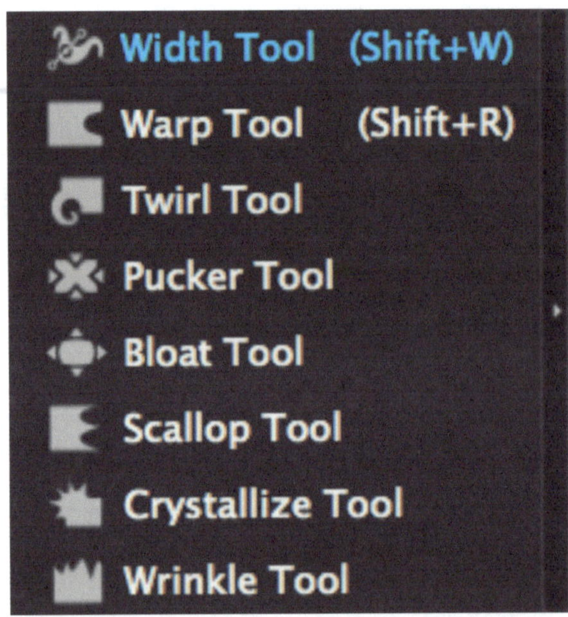

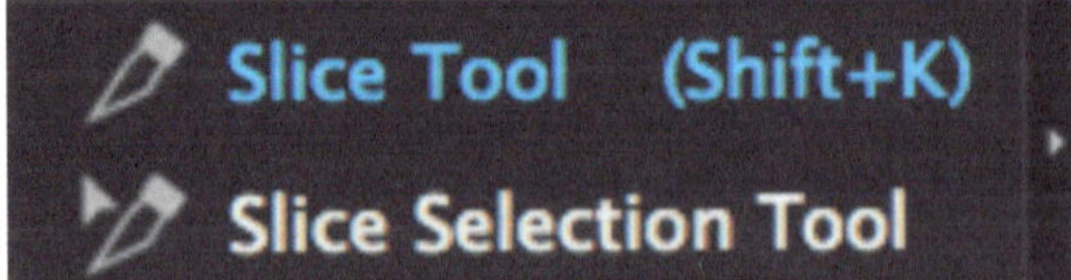

Slice Tool (Shift+K)
This allows you to separate your artboard into sections to save or export individually.

Slice Selection Tool
This allows you to select, change, move, and edit the slices you have made using the slice tool.

Width Tool (Shift+W)
This allows you to click on an area of a line and make the line stroke thicker or thinner.

Warp Tool (Shift+R)
This allows you to create warp effects on shapes and paths.

Twirl Tool
This distorts shapes by creating a twirl within them.

Pucker Tool
This puckers a shape creating a strong divot in them.

Bloat Tool
This bloats the selected shape, creating a bubble effect.

Scallop Tool
This works on shapes and lines and creates indents and bumps.

Crystallize Tool
This tool acts similarly to the scallop tool, but with larger indents and bumps.

Wrinkle Tool
This makes your shape or path wrinkled, adding bumps and wrinkles.

Expanded Tools

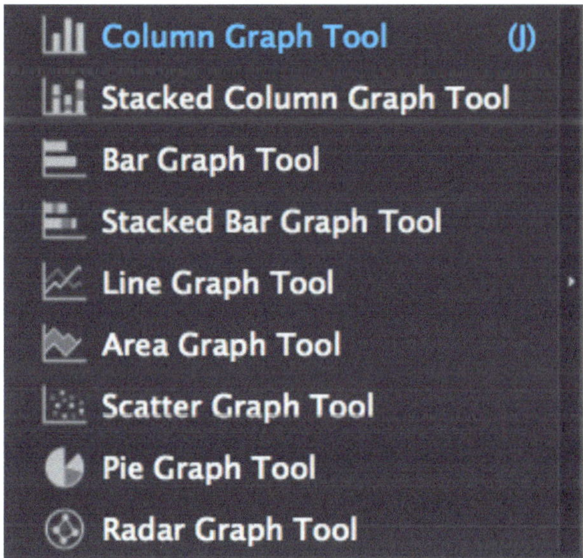

Column Graph Tool (J)

The column graph tool pops up a spreadsheet to input values to create a common column graph, which corresponds to values of the y-axis.

Stacked Column Graph Tool

This graph looks similar to the column graph, but the columns are segmented within itself, representing additional data from the chart.

Bar Graph Tool

A bar graph is a column graph facing horizontally instead of vertically, with the values of the bars aligning with the x-axis instead of the y-axis.

Stacked Bar Graph Tool

This bar graph includes segmented versions of each individual bar, to indicate more data than a typical bar graph does.

Line Graph Tool

A line graph uses points on the graph which are connected by a line.

Area Graph Tool

An area graph is similar in structure to a line graph but instead has shaded areas to include broader values of information.

Scatter Graph Tool

A scatter graph is made up of several points, scattered across the graph.

Pie Graph Tool

A classic pie chart where a circle is divided up into sections adding up to 100%.

Radar Graph Tool

A radar graph is similar to an area graph, but instead is round and can, therefore, have more variables than just two or four.

Expanded Tools

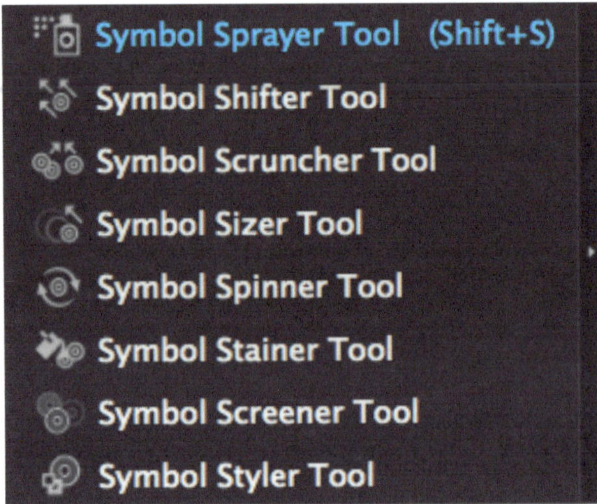

Symbol Sprayer Tool (Shift+S)

Open the symbol panel to select what symbol you want to be sprayed, then click and drag the spray can around your artboard to spray.

Symbol Shifter Tool

This tool allows you to move around symbols that have already been sprayed.

Symbol Scruncher Tool

This tool scrunches the symbols in towards the center.

Symbol Sizer Tool

This tool allows you to resize individual symbols after they have already been sprayed.

Symbol Spinner Tool

This allows you to rotate individual or multiple symbols at once.

Symbol Stainer Tool

This tool allows you to recolor individual symbols.

Symbol Screener Tool

This tool changes the opacity of individual symbols, making them lighter and lighter each time you click on them.

Symbol Styler Tool

This tool allows you to style your symbols more specifically by first using the Graphic Styles panel.

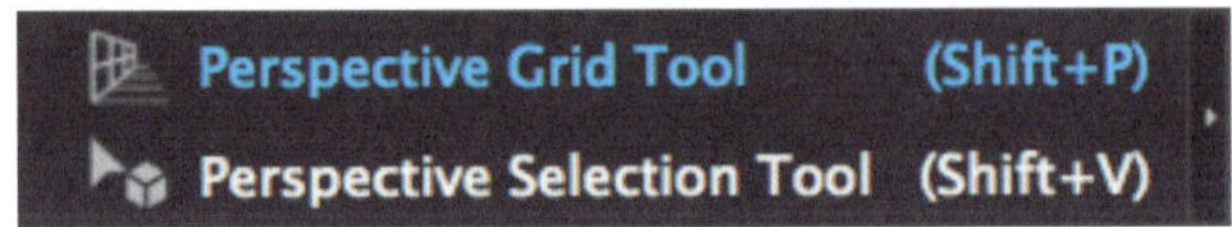

Perspective Grid Tool (Shift+P)

The perspective grid tool allows you to make your creations look 3D by giving them spatial awareness.

Perspective Selection Tool (Shift+V)

The perspective selection tool allows you to edit and change around the perspective grid that appears on your artboard. Select the three points that appear on the bottom of the grid, and slide them around accordingly.

TIPS

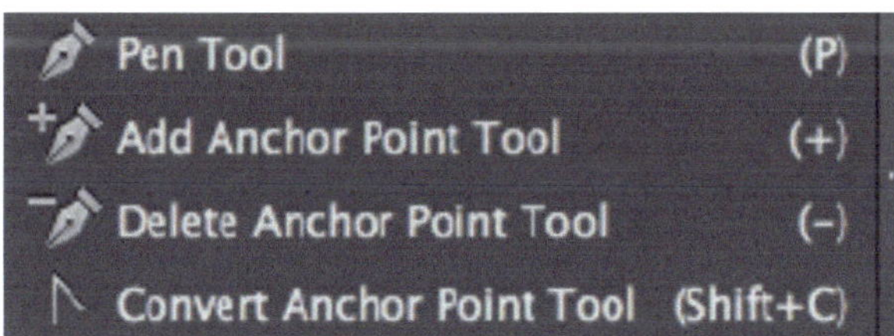

Click on this gray vertical bar to release these tools like below.

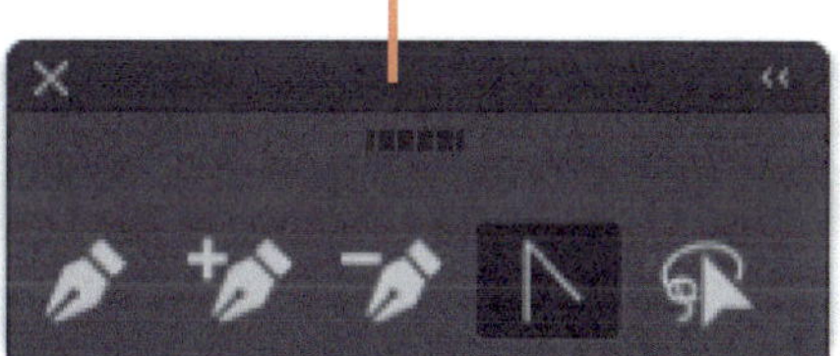

Click on these three dots at the bottom of the toolbar to open the editing toolbar area seen here.

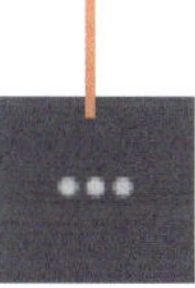

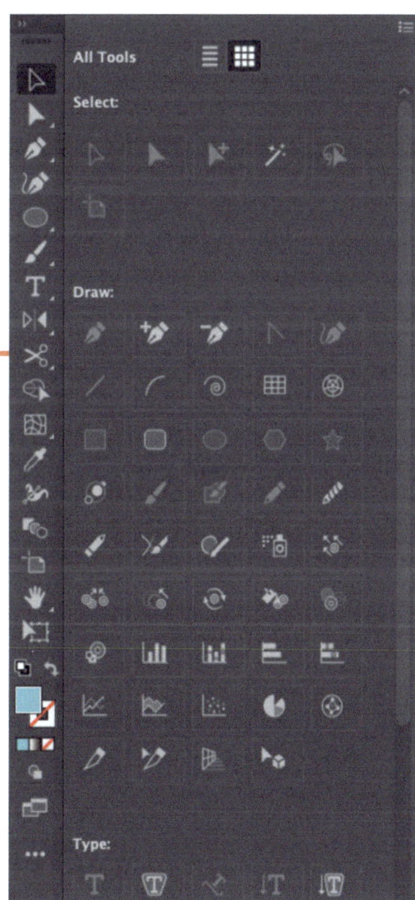

ABOUT THE AUTHOR

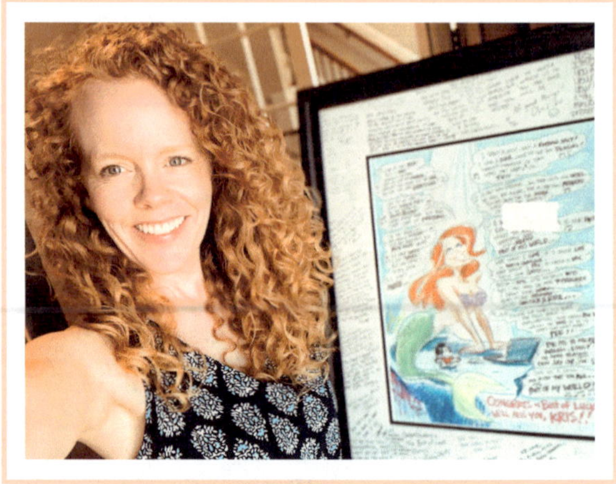

Kris Taft Miller

Kris joined Walt Disney Feature Animation directly out of college and spent eight years there, the first four in the Orlando studio and the remaining four in Los Angeles. She held numerous different types of roles in the Walt Disney Animation Communications department, including graphic designer, art director, producer, writer, presenter, and editor. Her film credits include *Lilo & Stitch, Treasure Planet, Brother Bear, Home on the Range, Chicken Little,* and *Meet the Robinsons.*

She moved to North Carolina in 2004 to be with her husband, Jeremy. She started her own graphic design company, KT Design, LLC, and continues to freelance for Disney, as well as a large variety of other clients around the world. Her specialties include book covers and layouts, e-learning, logos, web design, and countless print projects.

She also runs a successful educational materials line for elementary school teachers under her Print Designs by Kris.com label. She lives in North Carolina with her husband and two sons. Working on her own book projects, as well as her two sons' book projects, is one of her favorite things to do!

LET'S CONNECT.

Website: ktdesignacademy.com

Join the Facebook Community: @ktdesignacademy

Tag me with your design creations so I can see your design progress!
#ktdesignacademy

Made in the USA
Columbia, SC
29 November 2024